Fire Brigades of Merseyside

* * *

GW00601054

Fire Brigades of Merseyside

* * *

An Illustrated History

by

William R. Cockcroft

and

John D. Robertson

Foreword

by

Andrew E. Best Q.F.S.M., M.I. Fire E.

First published in 1993
© W. R. Cockcroft and J. D. Robertson

ISBN 0 903348 46 2

Typeset in Palatino by
Print Origination (NW) Ltd., Formby, Liverpool L37 8EG
Printed by The Cromwell Press, Melksham, Wiltshire SN12 8PH

Acknowledgements

The authors wish to record their gratitude to those many members of the local fire service who by their selfless devotion to public duty have made this record of their achievements possible.

They wish to thank the following people for their help and individual expertise so vital in the preparation of this book:

Andrew E. Best, Q.F.S.M., M.I. Fire E.
Chief Fire Officer of the Merseyside Fire Brigade
and the members of the
Merseyside Civil Defence and Fire Authority.

The staff of the Merseyside Record Office, Cunard Buildings, Liverpool.

Brian Dolan, B.A.,
Jim Gonzales,
Barbara Cockcroft,
Margaret Caulfield.
Tom Morley
Peter Withers

Sincere thanks, too, to all those who kindly subscribed to the book in advance.

Dedication

I dedicate this book to my wife, Edith Robertson in recognition of her patience and support through fifty one years.

J.D.R.

The Authors

John Denton Robertson was born in Liverpool in 1914. He became interested in the Fire Service as a boy scout, in 1924. On retirement from the Ministry of Transport he became the Honorary Archivist of the Merseyside Fire Brigade. He has compiled a unique photographic collection on behalf of the Merseyside Brigade and may be contacted through, Brigade H.Q., Hatton Garden, Liverpool, L3 2AD.

William R. Cockcroft, M.A., B.A., was born in Liverpool and has completed twenty eight years as a teacher and lecturer. He has written two other books – *'From Cutlasses to Computers, The Police Force in Liverpool, 1836-1989'* and *'The Albert Dock and Liverpool's Historic Waterfront'*.
He may be contacted at, 19 Bowness Avenue, Ainsdale, Southport, PR8 3QP.

CFO Andrew Best Q.F.S.M. M.I. Fire E.

Foreword

Andrew Best Q.F.S.M., M. I. Fire E.
Chief Fire Officer.

One of the earliest tools mastered by mankind was the use of fire. His ability to harness the heat and light of flame was considered a major milestone in the achievements of our species. One can imagine that the reproducing of the phenomenon, observed occurring in nature, was not easily learned and one can envisage early man frequently getting his fingers burned in his attempts to do so. His efforts were rewarded with a warm and dry cave, having its darkest reaches brightly illuminated, with the added bonus that this new tool also drove off the wild animals that stalked him in the night.

The benefits more than compensated for the occasional mishaps that must have occurred and so he persevered, developing the use of fire for cooking, for firing clay and for clearing the forest in order to give the land over to cultivation. Fire was the key with which man released metals locked in the earth; it also enabled him to fashion the metals to form tools and weapons.

Fire was used as a weapon in its own right and was so effective that the Romans formed VIGILUM units to combat the threat of attack by fire. These early fire brigades understood the principles of fire fighting and were skilled in the movement of water and in employing its use as an extinguishing medium. They were disciplined and well equipped having sophisticated pumps at their disposal. Their skills were lost on their departure from or absorption into, the communities that they had conquered.

As society progressed there was a tolerance of fire, and the occasional loss of someone else's life or property was accepted, much as were the unfortunate random victims of illness or disease. Such was the state of the nation when, as every schoolchild knows, a small fire broke out in the capital. The fire spread with such rapidity and ferocity that any attempts to tackle it were soon abandoned. It raged on out of control and is burnt into the nation's collective memory as the Great Fire of London, 1666.

This disaster awakened society to its vulnerability to outbreaks of fire and the lessons learnt produced changes in building practices and caused Parish Elders to rethink their arrangements for tackling fire.

The story is taken up by the authors of this well researched book which although it takes Merseyside as its point of focus, has general appeal deserving of a wider audience.

In the wake of Hollywood blockbuster 'Fire Fighting' films and the tremendously successful fire service television 'soap' series London's Burning, there is now great interest in the real fire service and in the real people who quietly perform their duty as proud members of brigades throughout the country.

This book 'Fire Brigades of Merseyside: An Illustrated History', is full, cover to cover with real people fighting real fires. The reader will almost feel the heat, taste and smell the smoke, but most important of all, will gain a true insight into the fire service in general and obtain an accurate picture of Merseyside Fire Brigade in particular.

I feel privileged to serve with the brigade and have great pride in proclaiming the professionalism and loyalty that I have witnessed in its members, at all levels, in both uniformed and non-uniformed serving personnel, past and present.

Andrew E. Best.

Contents

Part One:

The development of Firefighting on Merseyside.

Part Two:

The Illustrated History of the Brigades.

Chapter One

Parish Peace Disturbed

In the early nineteenth century the fragmentary development of local firefighting was very much in evidence on Merseyside. The impetus towards providing a more cohesive fire service originated chiefly within the rapidly expanding seaport of Liverpool. As its parochial organisation collapsed in the 1830s its councillors attempted to provide a series of fire preventative measures to protect its huge population and its vast municipal and private property.

Beyond its city boundaries there were some small-scale attempts by both private and voluntary groups to foster their own firefighting measures. In several of the nearby rural districts prosperous titled families, such as the Earls of Derby on their Knowsley Hall estate, financed their own brigades.

Their efforts also encouraged various nearby parish and village volunteers to band together and collect subscriptions in order to protect themselves. In the late Victorian period the West Derby Volunteer Brigade was known, for example, to have operated within the Wavertree, Huyton-with-Roby and Toxteth townships. Financed primarily by tradesmen and private householders this brigade became but one of many of its type that was formed throughout Merseyside.

Such brigades inevitably lacked the resources and organisation which wealthy boroughs like Liverpool had to provide to cope with the pressing dangers and increasing urbanisation. Even the efforts of the powerful insurance companies – some dating back to the Great Fire of London in 1666 – failed to provide all their clients with the level of protection they required. For several decades some of them, like the West of England Insurance Company, provided their brigade with their own distinctive uniforms, livery and insignia. They even attached company firemarks to those buildings owned by their clients. The success of their efforts, however, was undermined by the clamour to provide all Liverpool's citizens with protective fire measures.

The immense pressure upon the Liverpool corporation to guarantee such safeguards was brought to bear as the city became infamous for its lethal living conditions in the 1830s and 1840s. Near the borough's centre and in its overcrowded dockland districts the average expectation of life for many became a mere twenty years. Such a deplorable situation was not brought about by accident but was induced by unscrupulous landowners and builders who crowded as many persons as possible into the dwellings they erected. Land became scarce and as a valuable commodity especially near the docks, it was recklessly exploited.

The technology for firefighting in such over populated areas appears to have been woefully inadequate. In the 1830s and early 1840s, Liverpool, with a totally inefficient water supply, had the reputation of being the unhealthiest town in the United Kingdom. Unskilled persons and immigrants flocked there, especially by sea, and the dockland wards, like those of Vauxhall and Exchange became overrun by them. In these wards a dense mass of courtyard property was constructed to maximise the number of houses at the least possible cost. The courtyards were often cul-de-sacs of thirty to forty feet width surrounded by buildings. Many courts had an intermittent or a rationed supply of water delivered by carts. In the event of fire only the boldest of firefighters might enter the many 'death traps' of homes. Candles and naphtha oil lamps became widely used and when an accident involving serious injuries or burns occurred the journey to a local infirmary, such as the one in the city centre at Vauxhall Road, had to be undertaken. In many cases this was by means of a crude slow-moving stretcher or 'litter'.

Each crowded court apartment, often harbouring several families, would see many having to sleep on combustible shavings, or straw. Crude coverings might consist of newspaper wrappings or sacks. With few building regulations all occupants were placed at high risk by the widespread use of naked flames, particularly at night and in winter. These lights were commonly produced from the 'lucifer' matches which all persons including children, were encouraged to use. Young uneducated parents sought temporary escape from such conditions in the numerous outlets for drink such as the grog-shop, the beer-shop or the penny-ale cellar, which only added to the danger of fire from unoccupied property.

The recognised centres of every day work, both in the docks and town itself were often the centres of high risk because of the lack of basic fire and explosives regulations. The risks in warehouses were particularly great when vast amounts of inflammable goods such as North American cotton were stored. The import of raw cotton was the primary source of Liverpool's prosperity. The raw crops began to reach Liverpool around October and throughout the winter months until the following April poured into the port. This was especially so during the heyday of the wooden sailing ships and continued when steamships began to replace them. Even after sailing ships were eventually superseded in the final decades of the century, ship after ship arrived in the broad Mersey estuary laden with cotton bales to feed the hungry mills of Lancashire. Liverpool's early warehouse construction tended to promote fire outbreaks on a vast scale. In the seaport multi-storied warehouses were erected to house enormous departments that were found to be useless as fire-stops because builders had indiscriminately perforated them with doorways, hoists, shafts and windows.

When Liverpool's famous Goree Warehouses had burned in 1802, huge quantities of cotton, grain, sugar and coffee were ruined. An estimated £323,000 (early nineteeth century value) worth of goods was lost as the ruined stores continued to smoulder for 3 months.

Serious warehouses conflagrations were to recur throughout the first part of this century, despite the efforts of many responsible parties, including architects, engineers and firemen to improve their firefighting provisions. John Braithwaite, for example, had introduced his steam-powered fire engine pump in 1829 but few authorities were prepared to invest in his invention.

His second engine is reported to have been installed at one of the Liverpool docks but it was not until the 1860s that the power of steam for firefighting was recognised and sought after on Merseyside. Most local firemen continued to rely on their manual pumps until this decade. These hand or foot-powered devices frequently froze up in the cold winter periods and proved expensive and inefficient to operate at other times.

It was reported that an average size manual pump required some twenty men, ten on each side, to work. With few men being able to continue their exertions for more than a minute at a time, relays of teams became necessary. A minimum of forty men therefore might be required to work a twenty-man manual water pump.

As will be vividly shown, they were particularly handicapped at Liverpool's Victorian warehouse fires, when the local water source was inadequate. It became widely known, too, that while some manual volunteers shirked their responsibilities, feigning their pumping motions, others handled the equipment roughly and came to expect free beer refreshments be provided on a lavish scale.

As they plied their handles their cries of "Beer oh, beer oh", might rend the air. Some changed this to "no beer, no beer" if dissatisfied with the rate of the delivery of their expected beverages. In the same vein many of the volunteers would first insist they were given some means of identification, perhaps an arm band or a copper token, before taking on their duties. Nor was it unknown for trouble makers to interfere with the manual engines by cutting the lines of fire hoses.

In the early 1830s when the number of Liverpool's docks rapidly increased – eight new docks were built between 1815 and 1835 – the parochially organised firefighters could protect no more than about one third of the entire area of the borough. The city's improvement commissioners became convinced, following the recommendation of a former London Police Officer, Lieutenant Shipp, then employed in Liverpool, that one comprehensive fire force should be formed. They further urged that the insurance companies should be obliged to help with the cost of maintaining such a force.

Inspired by Shipp, the commissioners appointed a sub-committee to consider these recommendations. One of their body, Mr. Wales, obtained plans and estimates from a number of major cities. The various fire insurance agents, however, remained reluctant to support the cost of forming an independent fire brigade.

After another disastrous fire at Lancelots Hey, near the central docks, destroyed thirteen warehouses and nine dwelling houses, in 1833, a parliamentary bill to establish a city brigade was introduced by the parish watch commissioners. By December 1834, a 'fire police' force under superintendent William Gallemore was hastily established. Unfortunately the insurance offices had not pledged financial support for the force and their unwillingness to do so became a contentious issue that persisted well into the next century.

Further problems arose, too, when within a few months of its commencement other features of the force were criticised. The firemen presented an abnormally excessive bill for the Lancelots Hey fire with 5 of the captains and 28 of their firemen claiming they had each worked for 96 consecutive hours. The Watch sub-committee also condemned the men's bill for unlimited free refreshments. The insurance agents joined the chorus of condemnation of the new force believing that it was inferior to those in London, Glasgow, Edinburgh and Manchester.

In an effort to decide upon the contributions to be made by insurance companies, their spokesman, agent William Brown, travelled from London. He conferred with the commissioners and assisted in drafting a code of laws for the fire police and a scale of charges for those insurance offices willing to contribute. However, Gallemore was heavily criticised and then dismissed and replaced temporarily by Michael Whitty. The latter was the man destined to become Liverpool's outstanding first head constable, in 1836.

Following the passing of the Municipal Corporations Bill, in 1835, the Watch Committee proceeded to establish a borough fire department as part of the town's new police force. Quite apart from the economic advantage of saving on resources, Liverpool was to benefit from the firm control over unruly persons at fires by its own 'fire policemen'.

In April, 1836, John Hewitt was appointed foreman, or superintendent, of the fire brigade, at £100 per year salary. He was destined to become one of the region's outstanding fire chief heroes in the Victorian era. He was especially respected for his organisational skills and for working alongside his men in the worst of dangers.

Under his supervision the Temple Court fire station, boasting six manual engines, and six small water carts, became the city's headquarters. He directed that two firemen and a turncock be permanently stationed in each of the town's north and south police divisions. The new foreman also supported the need for a water cart, reel and hose to be kept in constant readiness at each station. Three manual engines were also on hand at those stations at the north end of the Prince's Dock, at the heart of Liverpool's transoceanic postal and passenger services. Two more manuals were kept in Lightbody Street and one for the hill-top outskirts of the city at Prescot Street.

These arrangements were the beginnings of the systematic deployment of resources that were to characterise Hewitt's strategies for firefighting.

Other nearby towns such as Birkenhead and St Helens also introduced noteworthy firefighting provisions at this time but they were small-scale arrangements compared to those of Liverpool. On the western banks of the River Mersey, Birkenhead formed its fire police in 1837. For many years, however, and in any major emergency, it looked to Liverpool for assistance.

To the east of Liverpool in St. Helens, plans for building a town hall, a courtroom and police cells were decided upon in 1838. Two years later a small contingent of Lancashire constables became operational in the township. By the end of the 1840s their auxiliary firefighting colleagues had two manual engines and a small assortment of water carts for any fire outbreak.

To the north-west, in the Southport region, there was only limited, voluntary brigade protection until after the middle of the century. Still somewhat difficult to travel to from Liverpool, its inhabitants traditionally looked to its neighbouring Lancashire towns for assistance. In 1845, for example, a horseman had to be sent to Ormskirk to summon help after a fire occurred on the Promenade.

Liverpool's newly formed municipal brigade, under John Hewitts' leadership had, in contrast to confront a series of major fires of fearsome proportions. Only two years after his appointment, Hewitt and his men had to face yet another calamitous warehouse inferno of quite remarkable magnitude. This occurred even though both Whitty and Hewitt had worked desperately hard to overcome some of the deficiencies they recognised. Having amalgamated the town and dock police forces, they realised that the dock policemen in comparison with those in the town were totally lacking practice as firemen. Since the most expensive fires took place at the docks, Hewitt had promptly added twenty constables to the dock division. He drilled them in the use of their equipment and paid each an extra 'fire police' shilling per week.

With so relatively few full-time firemen and with such basically crude and inadequate equipment at their disposal, the dockland fire, in Robert Street North, in October 1838, soon outstripped their admirable efforts. Once again, the prime cause for the rapid spread of the fire was the deficient water supply. This remained in private hands until 1847 in a period when it was not unknown for the poor to beg, steal, or fight daily for water in the streets.

When the firemen reached Robert Street North and placed stand-cocks in the fire plugs, no water flowed out and they soon exhausted that in their water carts. Hewitt eventually located an abundant supply of water for one engine at the nearby Leeds and Liverpool Canal, but the pressure proved too weak.

The inadequacy of their cumbersome equipment and the consequent difficulties it caused were repeatedly stressed by the head constable in his report. A hose carried to a warehouse roof did not work. At one point, Whitty himself fearlessly climbed on the roof only to find that the hose nozzle was not open. Superintendent Tyrell unscrewed this but it was too late.

"The branchman ignorant of the stoppage, had called out for the engine to 'play up' and in playing up, necessarily burst the hose, the water obtaining no other means of escape".

Even the Mayor attended to see if he could help. At one stage the firemen had twelve of their most powerful manual engines, in full play, yet they could only bring five hoses to bear on the fire because of the distance which the water had to travel from its source.

"The scene was one of indescribable alarm and confusion. All the warehouses in Robert Street, as well as the fine ones between the cotton shed and Waterloo Road, appeared at first doomed to destruction. The question being where it would stop, an explosion of salt petre in one warehouse was followed by a second explosion from the ruins, it was an awful one.

"We stood as it were under a dome of fire, flame, stones,

cotton bags and ignited missiles. The doors and windows of the houses in the adjoining street were either smashed or carried away, and all around appeared in flames. In this terrible emergency, the power at my command, more that one half of which had on any former occasion had been put under my requisition, seemed totally inadequate in the unexpected emergency".

This series of fires began at nine o'clock on Friday evening and Hewitt and his men did not extinguish it until six o'clock the following Sunday morning. Property destroyed was valued at £120,000. Both citizens and fire insurance agents were quick to complain after this fire about the efficiency of the fire department and the competence of its superintendent. The Watch Committee, however, exonerated both and even sought to help the force by equipping it with new and larger water wagons.

The entire municipal approach to confronting large-scale fires was to dramatically alter in Liverpool within the next ten years. The seaport was to provide an historic and monumental lead for other local authorities to follow.

When yet another horrendous dockland fire occurred, in 1842, in the waterfront district adjacent to Crompton Street, matters came to a head. City councillors and their wealthy business associates became intensely agitated by this latest of destructive and explosive warehouse fires. They admitted that whereas some fires had been started accidentially by careless seafarers and dock labourers, others they believed to be the work of loot-seeking incendiaries. Those merchants with properties in Crompton Street, Great Howard Street, Formby Street and Neptune Street saw much of it ruined. In 1842 they lobbied the local councillors to make the warehouse architects improve their designs and for the builders to introduce additional fire-proofing features.

The following year, when the contract to begin the Albert Dock was awarded they took note of the special fire proof features planned for the fortress-like dock. Jesse Hartley, the Liverpool Dock engineer had prepared and tested six different designs of warehouses between 1841 and 1843. His final choice of a brick and iron structure proved over-whelmingly resistant to attemps to destroy it by fire. Therein lay the immediate answer for the future – an unequivocal emphasis on fire prevention technology within new major buildings – an historic monument which still exists today as the Grade One listed series of buildings.

On 24th June the city magistrates asked the mayor to meet the Watch Committee members. In turn they agreed to provide a further fifty extra constables to act as a preventive warehouse patrol to discourage any would be arsonists. Thus the whole course of local warehouse building was significantly altered in a year that had also seen the passing of the Liverpool Warehouse Bill. This fundamentally provided for a system for the registration of all warehouses. With three categories of classification, those owners who had fireproof construction throughout their entire warehouses were to be offered the lowest premiums by the fire insurance companies.

A resolute group of these companies sought to tighten their grip on warehouse supervision when they initiated the formation of the Fire Salvage Association of Liverpool. They went on to organise the Liverpool Salvage Brigade. Included in this uniformed corps' responsibilities was the inspection of the seaports warehouses and the issuing of their own special certificate of approval. Their first certificate was awarded to the owners of Harboard's warehouse, New Quay, 2nd May 1844.

The Association had their offices and salvage equipment sited in Temple Street, close to the Central Fire Station, to show they were ready to act immediately upon any information they received about a fire brigade 'turnout'. This single-minded determination of these salvage operatives to protect insured property was left in no doubt.

The men of the Salvage Brigade, in their distinctive uniform, which included round flat-topped black leather hats inscribed with the golden letters 'Salvage' became a vital additional 'Watchdog' body. Under their bold leader,

Lieutenant Maxwell, inspector of salvage, they presented a new dimension in the fight against arsonists and looters.

Their expertise and reputation was to grow significantly throughout their one hundred and forty four year history. They were eventually invited, for example, to attend fires that had occurred outside Liverpool. Their expert scrutiny was particulary sought after in the cotton mill regions of Lancashire.

This development helped to compensate for the Liverpool Police fire department's lack of technical resources. With only three full-time firemen, sixty one part-time firemen and those casual labourers randomly recruited at the scene of fire there was an obvious need to organise a more professional body of men. The three permanent firemen, moreover, had to clean and repair all Liverpool's scattered equipment. Travelling by foot to do so they had to move the extremely cumbersome equipment weighed down by gunmetal fittings.

Their travelling time to the scene of a fire could often be critical in an era of relatively slow communication. With principal officer Hewitt living at the Temple Court headquarters, he was quite far from many of the docks. To summon all the firefighters he ordered his men to sound the alarm bell there for half an hour. Some no doubt needed this time to travel hastily from the police beats or their homes.

To increase the efficiency of 'pump', or fire-engine mobilisation, his drivers had to sleep above a stable adjoining Temple Court. They were expected to practice speedily harnessing any horses they needed from the ten kept there. Other colleagues were expected to pull those hand drawn carriages on which they transported their stand pipes, plug irons and up to 150 yards of hose.

When necessary they were also to make use of their special twenty ton water refill cart. Hence though such organisation was rather basic it was probably the earliest of its type for any municipal fire brigade on Merseyside. The problems arising from a shortage of suitable recruits for the police fire brigade, however, were set to continue.

Chapter Two

Raw Recruits
and
Liverpool Drill

The mid-1840s continued as extremely difficult years for Liverpool's Police Force, and its problems significantly hindered the efficiency of its fire department. Firstly, the department had come to terms, after the great warehouse fires of 1838 and 1842 with the deficiencies of the town's water supply. Next the inadequacies of its cumbersome equipment and the perennial shortage of satisfactory manpower was a continuing handicap. The enforced resignations of two of Liverpool's head constables, in 1844 and 1852 was a further blow to the morale of the police firemen. It was fortunate throughout this period that John Hewitt remained as the reliable foreman, or superintendent, in charge of the fire department.

The failure to recruit men of a suitable calibre lay rooted in the nature of the casual labour of many who lived in the great seaport. Dockland Liverpudlians by the score were plunged into poverty. In turn they usually had to seek employment on the docksides, principally as dockers, porters, carters, or as labourers building the warehouses or excavating the docks or new railways of the port.

Few with the exception of sailors, were sufficiently disciplined or physically fit to stay on continuous duty for extremely long periods. The best, until 1900, recruits were ideally taken to be those nimble, and courageous mariners who were in good health, reasonably intelligent and used to living and working in confined spaces, especially in the dark, at great heights and in inclement weather.

As for the rest, whether docker, bricklayer or plasterer, local work was regarded as 'seasonal', at the mercy of the trade winds prevailing upon the sailing ships or the economic vagaries of supply and demand when steamships began to replace them. Many had to meet the consequences of trade depressions such as that in 1841 in Liverpool. Hundreds of street beggars were taken into police custody as a result. In 1843, the police removed some 621 begging people from the seaport's streets, in 1844 a further 510 suffered a similar fate.

Those fortunate enough to find temporary work became salt-loaders, fruit-hawkers, street-crossing sweepers and the like but they never totally escaped from the trap of falling into periodic unemployment and poverty. The best the local authorities might hope for from such men was that the most able would travel to a fireface to act as casual recruits assisting the regular fire police. All such assistants usually readily accepted Liverpool's traditional refreshments of 'strong ale, cheese and bread'.

It was hardly suprising that many from this residual pool of labour indulged in the risks of causing fires on board ships or in the Liverpool warehouses. These outbreaks usually stemmed from their outright carelessness and ignorance. Policemen, in 1848, for example reported that in hundreds of instances warehouse employees had not locked their premises securely after work. Others smuggled pipes and matches into work, despite the dangers whilst working alongside cotton bales, timber and North American oil fuels stored in wooden casks.

In times of buoyant trade the River Mersey was crowded with sailing ships essentially constructed of timber frames and fittings. Tall masted deep sea barques and ships were tied up in almost every available dock. Whilst local sailors might view those craft made of English oak as ideal, others such as the celebrated Marco Polo, owned by the Liverpool Blackball line were built of highly inflammable Canadian pine. Such ships often carried high fire risk cargoes, too, such as timber and spirits.

Hundreds of small coastal craft, 'flats', schooners, gig boats and fishing trawlers were susceptible to fire. So great was the demand for sailing ship berths in Liverpool that Jesse Hartley, dock engineer from 1824 to 1860, transformed the port, doubling the number of docks and improving quayside fireproofing facilities. His developments, as mentioned above, included having immense new warehouses built at the Albert Dock, Stanley and Wapping Docks to receive high value and fire-risk cargoes.

It was hardly surprising that at this time many Liverpool citizens were extremely sensitive to the dangers of numerous fires. When Head Constable Miller left the port without any senior fire officer to safeguard it for an eight hour period, in 1844, he was dismissed.

His defence was that on this occasion the Birkenhead Watch Committee asked for his services and that of fifty of his men. The request was refused by the Liverpool Watch for they felt Birkenhead should use its own fire police force, formed in 1837, to cope. They felt Miller was required to keep order amidst the flood-tide of emigrants, or "the immense concourse of persons likely to be assembled at the pierheads, as well as to superintend the necessary arrangements for preventing accidents during the disembarkation from the various steam boats at night".

In the face of this prohibition, Miller flagrantly flouted the authority of his Watch Committee. He crossed the River Mersey at seven one morning and did not return to Liverpool until three in the afternoon. Setting an example of insubordination and neglect of duty to his men – since John Hewitt and a senior superintendent also accompanied him – the Watch Committee felt they had no other course than to ask him to resign.

Ironically, Miller had tried to assist Hewitt to improve the fire fighting abilities of his men. He continued to deploy his manual engines most systematically and had asked the Watch Committee to purchase lighter water carts, each capable of transporting 160 gallons. He also emphasised the need to have the carts permanently filled and have hoses for them kept at the ready so that they could arrive at an outbreak of fire before the manuals. Next he demanded pipe carriages, for moving spare hose, pipe-scaling ladders, crowbars, hammers, torches, keys, ropes and other vital equipment. Finally, to frustrate the fraudulent claims of the engine lever labourers he suggested that a copper engraving plate to produce 'time tickets' be purchased. Such a device helped the regular firemen to produce a supply of tickets limiting casual attendance to between one and six hours.

During this turbulent period the docklands continued to become heavily over populated and fraught with danger. Between 1845 and 1852, a former metropolitan police officer Maurice Dowling, held the office of head constable. He recognised the need for a firm approach "dealing with the large and populous neighbourhoods" that sprung up on the 'waste lands' as the new north docks and railway excavations attracted many thousands of navvies, or labourers. Many more districts became unbearably crowded as the immigrants – particularly the Irish – seeking passage out of Liverpool swept into the port.

Increasingly, the risks grew from the careless use of fire. Huge crowds assembled on a waterfront, embarking on cross ferry and trans-oceanic steamers. Many of the roughest and most desperate types sought employment there as fruit porters, lodging house touts, or luggage and merchandise haulers. Many known, former convicts worked in this manner as ticket- of-leave convicts. Was it surprising that at one point the Commissioner of Emigration had to be protected by Liverpool detectives after he had received written death threats, in his pierhead office, from the waterfront 'runners' or lodginghouse touts.

Dowling's fall from grace and his eventual dismissal from office marked the end of a somewhat distinguished police career. Until 1852 he had seemingly coped well with the unprecedented scale of Irish immigration, the expansion of Liverpool's docks and the shortage of recruits to join the police force. Dowling's lack of integrity in the scandalous Joughin case – whereby a sailor returning from Callao was robbed of 46 gold half-sovereigns by two prostitutes who falsely impugned licensee Charles Joughin – precipitated Dowling's dismissal.

This was a further blow to the morale of the long-serving members of the force and undermined their achievements. Dowling, for example, had been commended for his arrangements to protect Prince Albert, in 1846, at the opening of the Albert Dock. In addition he had encouraged, with Hewitt's support, an increase in the number of branch fire stations to seven. These were at Temple Court, Prince's Dock, Kirkdale, Rose Hill, King's Dock, Seel Street and South Haymarket. Firemen attached to these stations had a specific, adjacent district to be responsible for and they and other police colleagues placed prominent notices at street corners and on street lamp posts to direct the public to the nearest fire station.

Hewitt had steadily continued to promote the growing reputation of the fire department. In 1845 for example, his colleagues drove some of Liverpool's pumps to a fire at Crosby, a small township beyond the northern borough boundaries. While Hewitt became noted for his intrepid fearlessness at the scene of a fire, Dowling became intent on establishing a highly drilled and competent department so that each fireman became highly proficient in fixing fire apparatus or supplying water in any sudden emergency.

He insisted that this new drill be continuously practised as a constant supply of high pressure water became increasingly available in the town. Nevertheless, his men still had to use the water carts as late as 1848 as many of the proposed new water pipes had still not been laid. Prepared by his London police training, he went on to draw up explicit instructions that defined the duties of the entire force in the event of fire. Herein lay the basis for the future of Liverpool's growing firefighting professionalism.

Every fireman had to be able to operate the supply of piped water from the new Green Lane waterworks. Each had to be able to use the keys, and water release plugs, to fix stand pipes, roll out fire hose and understand the code of signals used with whistles when they worked with those turncocks able to use the special Liverpool, Bootle and Harrington water plugs. To help make these signals audible, senior police officers had to help supervise crowds at fires and keep them at a suitable distance from the firemen. This was in part to be achieved by the erection of barriers consisting of iron stanchions and cords.

He also had his fire department supplied with three suits of fire-proof clothing with attached breathing apparatus, as used in London. He believed these suits would enable his men to operate in dense smoke-filled locations without being overcome by fumes. He further ensured that each station was provided with its own fire-escape equipment. After each fire his sergeants had to examine these escapes and all the fire equipment as soon as it returned to its station and they were then to record any defects in a special book.

Before his dismissal, Dowling, ably supported by his fire chief John Hewitt, had continued to lay the foundations for a 'fire brigade' that was to emerge in the next two decades as the most exceptional in the region. However, the dismal conditions of work still persisted for the firemen and new and potentially lethal imports – enormous supplies of gunpowder and petroleum – had to be confronted.

Chapter Three

Gunpowder, Petrol
and
The Model Brigade

When John Greig succeeded the unfortunate Maurice Dowling as Liverpool's head constable, from 1852 to 1881, he too was plagued by the poor quality of the police recruits to all departments. Gunpowder and petroleum imports on a massive scale also began to endanger his firemen in an unprecedented way. The anxiety arising from these problems was partly alleviated by Greig because he enjoyed the first class support of John Hewitt until 1873 and afterwards that of John Hancox and George Copeland. They helped to oversee the introduction of the revolutionary steam-powered fire engines that were to make the brigade the best equipped on Merseyside.

In the 1850s even the most resolute of Hewitt's firemen faced enormous responsibilities that put their honesty and intelligence to the test. Many succumbed to overwhelming temptations to quit the fire brigade. Greig as his predecessors, had to dismiss members of the police force at an alarming rate. He did this to 161 constables in 1853, for example, and some of the reasons he recorded as 'drunk in a privy with a prostitute; filthy expressions towards the head constable; drunk on duty; absconding, bastardy warrant against him' and, 'off his beat in a public house smoking'. Some 153 constables resigned in this year, too, 'gone to Australia; gone home, a farmer; gone to sea;

and, gone to his trade a cabinet maker', were some of the reasons for doing so.

Their behaviour undoubtedly dismayed Greig but he realised that his men had exceptionally demanding duties. Police constables, including those from the fire department, invariably had to undertake unenviable tasks in public health work. They had to inspect the filthy and unwholesome lodginghouses and cellars; report to the inspector of nuisances the improper use of passages, streets or courts for the keeping of animals. Their obnoxious responsibilities included having to report daily whether those places used by contractors who removed and deposited the human waste or 'night soil' from the middens had been thoroughly washed out.

Their constant exposure to dangers from violence, accidents or fire also remained an everyday risk. In 1853 two constables met their deaths on the dockside. One drowned having fallen overboard whilst fighting a fire on the steam tug, Dreadnought, at the Kings pier; the other constable was stabbed and bled to death. So exhausting were their duties by this year, for the first time since 1836, they did not have to compulsorily attend a place of worship on each Sunday. Those with 12 months satisfactory service were also to be granted leave of absence with pay for 3 days in each year.

During the 1850s Greig and Hewitt struggled manfully to improve the confidence of Liverpudlians in their fire policemen. Whereas in 1851 Hewitt supervised 72 firemen in some 7 stations, by 1861 Hewitt had increased his command to 149 firemen operating from 17 stations. Of the latter, 9 were in the town including those at Hatton Garden – which in 1858 replaced Temple Court as the Headquarters – Athol Street, Essex Street, Jordan Street and Vauxhall Road.

At the dock stations his men were constantly alerted to the fire risks arising from the common practise of mooring four or five sailing ships abreast at the quayside. Hewitt readily accepted the duty of having his men enforce the bye-laws of 1854 to oversee the use of signal bells for extinguishing the fires and lamps used on board those vessels lying in the docks. With upwards of 15,000 sailors annually staying in Liverpool in this period constables had to be regularly assigned to extra duties at the docks.

Commendable though Hewitt's precautions to minimise the dockside fire risks were, his efforts were sometimes undermined by misfortune. In 1854 Hewitt had sent 18 constables on warehouse duty and supplied them with fire alarm rattles and whistles for signalling. A few months later he and his firemen were powerless to prevent flames from destroying the immense North Shore Cotton Factory and two nearby windmills that had granaries attached. Once again he felt the initial poor supply of water – the nearby canal having run dry at this incident – was to blame. Two years later he increased his constabulary strength at Clarence Dock to supervise the arrival and departure of disorderly passengers using the Glasgow steamers. In 1858 he also had to cope with disastrous burning of the mail, or packet, ship the James Baines whilst moored in the Huskisson Dock.

In the city, concern mounted as the coroner raised questions about the availability of police portable fire escapes after six persons had burned to death at a fire in Shaw's Alley near Salthouse Dock. A sub-committee appointed by the watch officials decided that the escapes in the borough were efficient enough. By the mid 1850s Greig reported that his men had fire escapes and other ladders at each of their eleven fire stations.

As more and more passenger and cargo carrying steamships entered the River Mersey by the end of the 1850s, the next decade was to become notable for the police fire department's reliance upon steam engine technology. Having experienced acute financial losses resulting from an inadequately equipped fire brigade at the time of the 1840's warehouse fires, efforts were intensified to prevent the like ever happening again. The merchants and brokers connected with the port were ever prepared to lobby the town councillors to protect their business interests.

In 1859 they demanded that the Liverpool Fire Prevention Acts of 1843 and 1844 be rigidly enforced to prevent the wanton carrying out of dangerous processes, or the careless storage of combustible articles in quayside buildings. William Rishton, the corporation's building surveyor approached the Watch Committee and they agreed to his proposals relating to the warehouses.

Greig in reponse to such fears, had Hewitt and his men inspect all Liverpool's warehouse property. He reintroduced the special patrols with a further instruction that the men so engaged rigorously report any persons who were storing combustible articles in prohibited places. They were also to search anyone suspected of smuggling tobacco into a warehouse. Under local by-laws tobacco had to be deposited in a safe place before entering a workplace, or office, and all lanterns had to be kept closed, locked and maintained in a satisfactory condition.

Senior fire officers also grew concerned during the early sixties, the period of the American Civil War, 1861-65, about the careless way in which gunpowder consignments were moved about the River Mersey, and through the city of Liverpool itself. Arms and ammunition store houses for the volunteer corps of the borough were poorly sited. The firemen expressed their support for an improved system for safeguarding explosives after a fire broke out, 16th November 1861, at a cigar factory, 78 Duke Street. The front cellars of the building were occupied as an armoury for a company. During the fire their twelve barrels of ammunition had to be removed to the south dock police station for safety. Greig suggested that such a store might in future be best sited at the North Fort, in Seaforth.

Even those gunpowder vessels anchored in the River Mersey were unsafe. One of them, the Lotty Sleigh, exploded whilst in the Sloyne off Tranmere, in 1864. With eleven tons of gunpowder aboard it caused extensive damage on both sides of the river. Following this traumatic experience a Liverpool river police department was formed and provided with three six-man gigs, or rowing boats. By this means Liverpool policemen could be sent to supervise any conveyance of gunpowder by ship or barge. On the river they had to ensure that any storage was kept beyond special limits.

River policemen had to stay aboard any vessel discharging, or taking on, gunpowder. On such craft fires were prohibited until the vessel sailed. Those storing gunpowder whilst in the seaport could only do so now in small quantities since bulk stores had to be kept aboard floating magazines – off Rock Ferry and Egremont – beyond the borough boundaries.

It was not until the 1870s however, that the railway companies agreed not to send any gunpowder supplies, beneath the city, through their Wapping and Waterloo dock tunnels. Instead they forwarded their consignments direct from Edge Hill Station overland down to the river's edge at Garston and had vessels ship them out to the estuary magazines.

Growing fears were similarly expressed about the dangers posed by the increasing import of North American petroleum, or 'rock oil' or 'earth oil', in the seaport. John Baker Edwards, Professor of Chemistry at the Royal Infirmary urged, in April 1862, that greater legislative protection needed to be sought to protect members of the public from petroleum evaporation from wooden storage casks.

From his laboratory at Liverpool's Royal Institution he declined to accept the Watch Committee proposal that he examine the inflammable and explosive properties of petroleum. He believed the temperatures of a burning building could not be imitated on a small scale and that "an adequate idea of the intensity of combustion could not be obtained in a safe experiment".

A large scale fire, in contrast, would be too unpredictable if it involved the true conduct of petroleum in wooden casks. Instead, he enclosed an account of the burning of a factory in Detroit, U.S.A., from the Detroit Advertiser, 4th April 1862. The verbatim reports of this helped to convince the Liverpool authorities of petrol's lethal potentialities.

Verbatim report from the Detroit Advertiser 4th April 1862.

"Explosion of a Kerozene Oil Refinery in Detroit

About 15 minutes past 10 yesterday morning the city was startled by the sound of a large report resembling the simultaneous discharge of a battery of artillery ringing through the air. Buildings were shaken to their foundations; windows broken and furniture thrown down and in some houses destroyed... a dense column of smoke rose up through the air in the vicinity of the water works house which was succeeded by the bursting of a sheet of flame at the oil refinery of J. H. Harmon and Co. situated near the corner of Dequinder and Alwater Street. The entire roof, the building and a portion of the walls were lying scattered around, and a most intense fire raged amid the flames."

That some four persons were killed by the Detroit explosion and 15,000 dollars worth of property was destroyed served to show that Liverpool councillors might again have been risking the type of 1840's warehouse devastation they had experienced. John Baker Edwards, in conclusion, felt the only means of control at the disposal of the firefighters was limited to "an abundant supply of water" which they had no option but to apply in the usual way at an early stage. It was later recognised that the use of water at a petrol based fire was inappropriate and that flames had to be smothered by use of an inert gas, or foam, to exclude oxygen.

Although unable to conduct a large scale experiment Baker made a report upon the nature of the four distinct burning fluids imported into Liverpool. He believed that of Petroleum, American Benzole, Kerosoline and Kerosene, petrol or 'natural rock oil' was the most threatening, arriving in the port in enormous quantities and in its raw state being used for lubricating machinery. He added that shippers of these fluids should replace their wooden casks by light iron casks or tanks.

Such was the fear aroused by the dangers presented by these imports that new bye-laws for regulating the storage of petroleum and its dangerous by-products were in force by September 1862. One month later, under the Act for the Safekeeping of Petroleum, Act 25 and Act 26 Vict., cap 66, any person seeking to keep petroleum had to apply for a licence to do so. It was reported to the Select Parliamentary Committee of 1866 that Liverpool was the only city that had made any provision for the safe storage of paraffin. In other cities thousands of gallons of such continued to be stored in the same warehouse compartments as jute and cotton.

Nevertheless, accidents with petrol did occur from time to time in Liverpool. In January 1864 at 106 London Road petrol vapour escaped from the Thomas Oil and Colorman, retail shop. Mr. Thomas the owner luckily escaped with the hat burned off his head and his hair singed. John Hewitt attended the incident promptly with a fire engine and crew but they were not required.

The determination to provide the best protection possible against fire outbreaks made Liverpool's Watch Committee the most resourceful in the region in this period. They had made a further step, in August 1861, when they recommended that a Shand Mason steam-powered fire engine be purchased. Greig and the redoubtable Hewitt had initially inspected both the land and the river steam fire engines used in Watling Street by London's Metropolitan Fire Brigade. Each engine had performed magnificently at the great fire in Tooley Street 22nd June 1861, in the capital.

On Greig's advice the Watch Committee recommended to the Council that a land, steam-engine be purchased at £600. It was much cheaper than the converted London steam tugboat or river engine priced at £4,700 and Hewitt's men could comfortably have fitted it on board a vessel and used it as a floating fire engine to tackle any river or dockside fire. Until this time when a fire broke out on a ship in the river or in the docks, a steamship had been requistitioned by the fire police and they had their manually operated fire engines taken on board. Driving a horse-drawn, steam-powered fire engine aboard a steamship meant that they would have been able to increase the speed at which they were able to operate against a vessel on fire. They would not have been held up by recruiting labourers for manual fire engines. This could have been the first 'float' or river fire boat on Merseyside completely dependent upon steam.

Along the line of docks the engine could have been fed with a dam of water from any wet dock. Complete with coal and water, the engine weighed nearly three tons. The firemen filled its boiler with cold water and fed its fire with wood and coal. The men were also capable of raising a seven-eighth inch jet of water from it to nearly 130 feet. Was it ever put to use in Liverpool? It appears not to have been approved of by the Council because four years later a Merryweather steamer, not a Shand Mason, was purchased for the Liverpool Brigade.

After John Hewitt's London visit he and his men continuously sought to introduce other improvements. They replaced their tall constabulary 'top hats' in 1864, with helmets. In 1865 the steam-powered engine the 'Clint' was purchased for £650. A contract for horsing the fire engine was granted, Hewitt had a special class of fire stokers trained and jets of gas were applied to the engine's boiler to quicken the rise of steam pressure. Greig, in 1872 applied for another engine having found the first able to cope with 'any fire'. He sought to prevent a disaster in the event of it ever 'breaking down'. The firemen experienced such a fate with 'The Clint', in

March 1873. Returning from a fire at St. Michael's Church, West Derby Road, a rear wheel gave way at the bottom of the steep London Road hill and the men had to store the engine in the yard of the London and North Western Railway in Lime Street.

In contrast, the Watch Committee was reluctant for many years until 1872 to introduce the telegraph system to improve firefighting. When they did so Greig felt that any part of the city, particularly the north end where there were petroleum sheds, timber yards, and a large tonnage of steam shipping, could be quickly served by Hewitt and his steam engine crews in the event of fire. When a new contract for horsing engines was drawn up, in 1877, George Copeland, Hewitt's successor, could call upon three engines – The Clint, 1865, The Livingstone, 1873, and The Hamilton, 1874. Liverpool's firemen, who cared for these engines and their horses with great pride, thus began to rightly regard themselves as an elite corps or model brigade within the police service. To enter this department each man was now required to serve his time as a probationer.

The department's horse contractor was also required each day to provide six suitable horses, to be left in the care of two efficient drivers, at the Hatton Garden Stables, from 7am to 7pm. For night duty such horses were left with three drivers, from 7pm to 7am. On some occasions the strain of a desperate gallop to a fire took its toll. In April 1877 one gallant horse dropped dead in Woolton whilst pulling a fire engine to a Halewood fire. After the firemen had extinguished any fire they had to speedily withdraw their horses and equipment so that the Salvage Corps could take complete charge of any clearance operations.

By the 1870s the firemen had won for themselves a fine reputation, particularly after helping in such localities as Bootle and Sefton Park, which were just beyond the Liverpool borough boundaries. Liverpool's own citizens were invited to attend regular public displays of the Brigade's prowess. In

August, 1873, for example, steam fire engine trials were staged in front of the Free Library in William Brown Street, adjacent to St. George's Hall. It became a regular feature for the men of the brigade to twice yearly wash each borough statue with high pressure jets of water. After 1870 an experienced fireman, too, was stationed inside each large theatre or building when large public gatherings took place.

It was hardly surprising that local newspaper reporters recorded the high regard of Liverpool's citizens for this branch of the police force. The Porcupine had proclaimed on 9th November 1867.

"One branch of the Liverpool Police Force is particularly deserving of high recommendation, the Fire Brigade. As a general rule, the body may be set down as the elite of the force. They are men of remarkably fine physique, and to judge by their coolness and intrepidity in facing danger their mental idiosyncrasy is equal to their bodily strength and agility".

The high standard was also reflected in their record of achievements. Greig in his annual report, 1871-72, was able to remark that there had been fewer fires in that year than for any of the previous twenty years. By 1872 Liverpudlians could count 19 fire stations spread across the seaport, with 13 in the town and 6 at the docks. Each of these too, were in contact, except for that at the Brownlow Hill workhouse and the Battery Street and Salthouse dock stations, by telegraph. Liverpool's exemption from large fires, Greig believed had chiefly resulted from this system of rapid communication and the city's efficient water supply. The longest period they had needed to use a steam fire engine at this time had been for 14 hours at the fire aboard the barque John Fyle in the Prince's Dock.

By the 1870s as other fine municipal brigades began to emerge across the United Kingdom several of Merseyside's smaller borough brigades were handicapped by their paucity of resources and equipment. This situation persisted for them until the final decades of the century when improvements were spurred on by the Public Health Act, 1875.

Chapter Four

Who Pays the Fireman?

The requirements of all Merseysiders to accept that the control of fires was a public duty was finally enforced by the Public Health Act of 1875. This embodied the first general legislation, relating to this obligation, that was neither permissive nor adoptive.

Many local authorities had at this juncture to look enviously at the firefighting arrangements in the major cities such as Liverpool, Manchester and Salford and to those smaller towns including Ashton-under-Lyne, and Tynemouth, which by virtue of their local acts had obtained the power to charge their ratepayers for fire brigade protection.

Liverpool's reputation for fire prevention also grew as the city boundaries expanded to encircle hitherto unprotected districts. In other parts of Merseyside the common use of phosphorous friction matches, town gas for lighting and for fuel, and the use of oil lamps, in the rural communities led to more anxiety. In many homes the increased popularity of tobacco smoking and the wearing of crinolene dresses were further new fire risks.

Extra industrial processes even in the small town communities such as Great Crosby and Birkdale meant that dangerous fire using activities in congested back streets were a serious hazard. These problems were magnified in the larger townships of Bootle and St. Helens where mills, factories and other industry sprang up adjacent to heavily populated dwelling house districts.

Though each local authority had become bound by the

Public Health Act, 1875, to provide a sufficient water supply for firefighting, a wide variety of fireplug hydrants was used across the region. Co-operation by neighbouring authorities might still therefore be frustrated by the lack of standardisation.

By the 1870s the majority of Merseyside's Victorian fire brigades had been fashioned almost entirely from their own local resources. Southport, for example, used a horse-drawn manual which it had purchased from Oldham in 1862.

Bootle, too, had sought help from Lancashire by asking the County's head constable, Colonel Bruce, to assist in establishing a small, municipal police fire brigade in 1870. One inspector and six constables equipped with some basic apparatus – including reels, hose, hydrant pipes, fire keys, axes, ropes, ladders and a London style wheeled-carriage, fire-escape – found it increasingly difficult to cope with the growing demands of the heavily industrialised dockland area of the borough. From time to time it was forced to enlist aid from Liverpool's fire department or from the dependable West of England Insurance Brigade. Like St. Helens, Bootle struggled until the 1880s to cope with the excessive demands that finally forced before the end of the century, a much needed reappraisal of its firefighting provisions.

Beyond the boundaries of Merseyside's boroughs large stretches of countryside still remained relatively unprotected. The risks increased as the railways were constructed into Liverpool's hinterland and transported more and more travellers into it after the mid 1840s. It was not unknown for many thousands to leave their mid-Lancashire industrialised towns for the coast, especially on Sundays, by this popular method of mass cheap travel.

In the main the rural areas came to rely upon volunteer fire brigades. An outbreak of fire might see church bells or bugles being used to summon the men to action. To clear their way, rythmic shouts, post horns or bugles would be used. In some brigades, following Liverpool fire department's example, the entire crew might each blow a whistle in unison as a warning. Apart from the West Derby Brigade, volunteer corps were known to exist in Birkdale, c.1876, Crosby and Blundellsands, c.1880, Formby, c.1898 and Wallasey, c.1898. Others operated in Hightown, Hoylake, Huyton and Maghull.

Throughout the region beer was still provided as a post-fire refreshment. In Liverpool it was especially supported by the powerful brewer interest which was well represented on the city council. By this period however, it was the custom to use only a respectable public house as a venue for the men to drink and to recuperate. This was still regarded as acceptable by the public in an era when the firemen – and their Chief Officer in particular – were regarded as a heroic figures worthy of the admiration of the Royal Family.

Unfortunately, fire station facilities in even the best borough brigades were often scandalous. Many men were expected to sleep in their only uniform in a confined space with just a single blanket in Winter for cover. On duty for as long as 60 hours at a time, sometimes without removing their belt or axe, they were expected to unquestioningly put their life at risk in a variety of situations. The lot of the fireman, like that of his constable colleagues was often not a happy one.

Which was the best way to organize such obedient firefighters? This continued as a burning issue for many years. In 1876, the Select Committee reporting on the Metropolitan Fire Brigade focused on the two main fire brigade systems in large towns. Some municipalities such as Glasgow, Manchester, Salford and Edinburgh favoured independent fire brigades. Others such as Liverpool, Leeds, Sheffield, Bristol, Bradford, Nottingham, Hull and Newcastle combined their police and fire brigade responsibilities.

Across the country, councillors, parish representatives, insurance agents, policemen and firemen became divided in their opinion as to the most effective form of organisation for firefighters. Liverpool, as Greig had testified before the Select Committee on the Metropolitan Fire Brigade, in 1862, was well satisfied with its highly regarded police fire brigade. Yet whilst he was supported by London's Richard Mayne and several other distinguished policemen, many other senior constables such as Lieutenant Colonel Henderson, opposed any unification of the police and firefighting services.

Mayne and those colleagues who supported his viewpoint felt strongly that the protection of life and property from fire was as much the duty of the police as was the preservation of the public from criminal harm. Henderson in contrast, believed that the additional responsibility for firefighting would limit a policeman's effectiveness in preventing crime.

Some city fathers and local businessmen promoted a police fire brigade simply to save on the expense of providing separate resources for firemen. They concluded that for the same, or only a little extra outlay, their policemen should play a dual role. After 1856 this arrangement had appeared particularly attractive, for there was a government grant available for police forces after this year but not for independent fire brigades.

Others voiced determined opposition to the joint system. Members of the Works and General Purposes Committee of London's Metropolitan Board of Works were appalled, in 1875, by the suggestion that the control of the Metropolitan Fire Brigade should be taken away from the Board of Works. The Committee members argued that the admirable efficiency of both Liverpool's and Manchester's firefighters was down primarily to the fact that their local water supply was under the control of the respective city corporations. If a police brigade authority could control the water supply it had the power to levy rates. In this case the local ratepayers would not be represented since the Metropolitan Police finances were administered by the government and the ratepayers had no control over such expenditure.

Was it surprising then that after 1876 Metropolitan London continued to operate the system? Captain E. M. Shaw, the superintendent of the Metropolitan Brigade and one of the most famous of Victorian fire chiefs favoured this separation even though he – like Liverpool's early chief fire officers in the 1840s and 1850s – found great difficulties in recruiting firemen. Shaw attributed this situation principally to the poor conditions of work he had to see his firemen endure. Their pay was hopelessly inadequate, some of the men had to be kept on 'alert' for 24 hours each day and they had no superannuation fund. However, having personally examined the fire service in several large British cities and some of the mainland of Europe, including Paris and Berlin, he still wished to retain the Metropolitan system.

The perennial inability to resolve the question of the financial contribution of the fire insurance companies, added to the perplexity of the situation. In Liverpool insurance company payments had remained constant since 1864, whilst the expenses of the corporation for funding the brigade had doubled. Nott-Bower vociferously called for review of this contribution. Any examination was bound to be complex since the history of this payment was a long and involved one.

During the years 1863, 1864 and 1865, this had been frequently discussed. The Watch Committee had become completely dissatisfied with the sum paid, much correspondence took place and many discussions had been held between the committee members and the representatives of the companies. One consequence was that in December 1865, the companies had agreed to backdate an increase in their contribution from 1st April 1864, from £350 to £650 per annum.

By 1873, John Greig felt £650 to be inadequate. For the next ten years many demands for an increase failed. In contrast the companies agreed to pay towards salvage operations – such as the three pence per hour for each waterman and fireman engaged amounting to £373.00 in 1883 and £595.00 in 1884. On 1st September 1883 the secretary of the fire office committee, H. E. Hall, working at 11 Queens Street, Cheapside, London, explained that his members had resisted any increase "so long as the powers given to your (Liverpool) Corporation by their Act of 1842 are enforced in the partial manner in which they are at present exercised".

Committee members felt justified in refusing to increase their payments since nearly half of those insurance companies operating in Liverpool did not make a contribution to the corporation's fire department's costs. Whilst 21 companies made contributions some 18 did not. The contributing companies were; Alliance, Atlas, Caledonian, Church of England, Commercial Union, Guardian, Imperial, Lancashire, Manchester, North British and Mercantile, Northern, Norwich, Phoenix, Queen Royal, Royal Exchange, Scottish Provincial, Scottish Union and National, Sun Union, Westminster, West of England and Yorkshire. The following companies did not contribute; Building Society and General, City of London, Equitable, Fire Insurance Association, Glasgow and London, Hand in Hand, Kent, Law Union, Lion, London and Provincial, Midland Counties, Mutual, National of Ireland, Start Bowkett, and General and Lloyds.

In an attempt to bring matters to a head, the Liverpool Watch Committee had a notice inserted in local newspapers, the Courier, Mercury, Post, Albion and Journal of Commerce, warning that after 1st August 1885, the provision of the Liverpool Improvement Act 1842, with reference to the recovery of expenses of fires, would be enforced against those insurance offices as did not join in the payments made by other offices to the Corporation.

The sums authorised to be recovered by the Act were, firstly the wages of the fire police in addition to their allowances for the occasion, secondly, the pay of further assistants necessarily employed, thirdly, the cost of the wear and tear of engines, utensils and those expenses incurred by damage and injury sustained at fires.

Across the country the procedure for levying charges for the expenses of firefighting forces costs varied greatly. In London, in the Metropolitan Board of Works district the contributions were regulated by section 13 of the Metropolitan Fire Brigade Act, 1865, this laid down that each insurance compay was to pay annually to the Board of Works a sum "after the rate of thirty five pounds in one million pounds the gross amounts insured by it".

In the Midlands, the boroughs of Leicester provided a complete contrast. Only one contribution of three guineas, from a single office was received each year. In Nottingham no contributions at all were paid. In Birmingham, too, none of the insurance companies made a fixed contribution, but a small sum or donation was paid with respect to fires on premises insured by the offices. Wolverhampton's insurance companies met the bare cost of extinguishing fires occurring on insured premises.

Manchester, unlike Liverpool, did not have any power for extracting contributions from the insurance companies. By the Manchester Town Hall Improvement Act, 1866, the owners of property endangered by fire became liable to contribute "the actual expenses incurred by the corporation in the establishment and maintenance of the fire brigade, and for the use of engines, implements and apparatus, and for the water for the purpose of salvage". The insurance companies, however, voluntarily contributed to the expenses of the fire brigade, until March 1884, the Corporation then began to recover the expenses from the owners of the endangered property, according to the scale of charges linked to the value of the property.

In view of the reluctance of so many insurance companies in Liverpool to make a suitable payment, George J. Atkinson, the town clerk proposed "a scale of charges similar to those imposed in Manchester". In the event of a dispute between Liverpool Corporation and the property owners, the amount as in Manchester was to be decided by two magistrates.

The question of funding an adequate fire service was to remain a complex and unanswered one until the middle of the twentieth century. The large and wealthy corporation of

Liverpool struggled to find a satisfactory method of raising monies to pay for its firefighting establishment in the Victorian era. How much greater then was the burden placed on the smaller and much less affluent local authorities on Merseyside during the same period?

True, the scale of the threat of fire was considerably higher in Liverpool than in other towns of Merseyside. Municipal concern for deliberately started fires, for example, was constant throughout this period in the seaport – particularly at the docks. Fires ignited for political motives – such as those of the fanatical Irish Republicans, the Fenians, in the 1880s – further honed the brigade's specialist knowledge of explosives. Following the near successful attempt in 1881 to dynamite the Town Hall and a Hatton Garden Police section house further outrages were attempted the following year. Large canisters filled with lignine dynamite, with fuses and especially constructed taps to act as timing controls, were, fortunately intercepted before 'Fenian's Fire' or small bombs could be employed in a similar fashion. In 1881 the replacement of the telegraph system by one using telephones, undoubtedly helped the Liverpool Fire Brigade to improve its communication of vital messages.

Several neighbouring townships did make notable steps to improve their provisions for firefighting in the 1880s. In 1880 St. Helens had opened a fire station in Parade Street. Two full-time firemen were employed in a building which housed a horse-drawn hose carriage, stables and, eventually, a horse-drawn steam engine, too.

By 1883, Bootle also proudly displayed its steamer 'Bootle' as the means of permitting its men to tackle some of the largest fires they had to encounter. By 1886, it became apparent that further improvements were vital and a more professional brigade was organised. Captain G. W. Parker took command thereon of two permanent firemen, fifteen auxiliaries, the steamer and a Hall manual engine. The latter was painted blue and vermilion and named The Pioneer.

Southport also boasted, by 1900, a police fire brigade which was equipped with a steam engine, a hose carriage and an 'escape' van. The need to improve the working conditions and facilities for even the best equipped borough brigades still remained.

Chapter Five

Go home and change, the fire is out

In his seaching report of 1892, Liverpool's head constable, William Nott-Bower, concluded that the city's Fire Brigade was excellent value for the revenues spent on it. It had the reputation by the last decade of the nineteenth century of being one of the best equipped and best organised units in the United Kingdom. The men of the brigade, however, still had to endure some of the most wretched of working conditions at their fire stations.

Superintendent James Willis was required to live at the antiquated headquarters in Hatton Garden and ensure that the fire engines, reels, escapes and other vital equipment was kept in perfect working condition. In strict rotation, he visited all the district stations, drilled their regular firemen and instructed new recruits how they should use the array of firefighting appliances. When he heard the fire alarm bell he had to determine the scale of the fire and unhesitatingly order a steamer to any outbreak that occurred in a sailing vessel, a warehouse, a timber yard, a theatre or any other major public building.

His two deputies had to live in the centre of their individual territorial districts. These each covered approximately half of the city. In turn these superintendents were obliged to accompany those dock firemen who were responsible for examining the vast number of hydrants and appliances, which were needed to protect all the city's principal public buildings and warehouses. They also had to ensure that the steam engines were meticulously maintained by the brigade's four highly experienced engineers.

Since there were only seven full-time fire officers and nineteen full-time firemen of lesser rank they had to rely upon the support of the auxiliaries. The latter consisted of sixty six firemen-turncocks, and eighteen 'escapemen'. These two groups were permanently assigned, in teams of three, to each of the twenty-two district stations and six fire escape stations. Each firefighter was selected primarily for his qualities of intelligence, stamina and forebearance. With one of the team on duty for a minimum of eight hours each day it guaranteed that one man at least was available every twenty four hours in the event of a fire.

Should the police constable determine the fire was a considerable distance from the station, or if it was frightening in nature, he could summon a horse-drawn carriage, ride upon its outer box and shout the alarm as he travelled. Any constable successfully taking the alarm to the station might later claim a shilling reward.

Police auxiliary firemen arriving at a fire might also anticipate a further reward, or 'fire bonus'. They each placed their own special talley inside a box, mounted on the brigade's first turn applicance to claim an attendance award of two shillings and sixpence. As soon as the fire was under control the officer in command ordered the closure of the talley box. Such bonuses were paid in addition to the extra two shillings and sixpence per week that constables received for their general firefighting responsibilities. When a fire was finally extinguished, or if the alarm was false, each constable had to immediately pass on either a message, "the fire is out" or "no fire". Those called upon to help with any salvage operations had to ensure that their times of duty were recorded by the superintendent in charge of fire operations.

After they had attended a fire they could be ordered to

return immediately to their police beats – even if they were in a bedraggled state. Only when 'dripping wet' might they expect to receive their orders to "go home and change" their clothes. If unable to do so they might be allowed to use one of the two large fire grates in the Hatton Garden police section house, to dry out their clothes. The largest grate at other times was used mainly for roasting joints of meat or for keeping food warm.

Such inadequacies at the Hatton Garden headquarters – in use by the fire department since 1858 – lay in the outmoded design of the building. It incorporated at this time engine houses, a hose drying tower, workshops, a smithy, stables, van houses, offices and the telephone room but Nott-Bower insisted that they should also have lavatories, a dressing room, a reading and recreation room for ordinary firefighters as well as homes for the officers. Most importantly, too, it lacked bathrooms, so vital for those regularly exposed to dirt and inclement weather.

He forcefully maintained that there was probably no large city in the United Kingdom so badly provided for in this respect as Liverpool. Fine examples of model fire stations by contrast were the headquarters of the Metropolitan Fire Brigade in Southwark's Bridge Road, or on a smaller scale, the fire station of the Borough of Leicester, and the station of the Liverpool Salvage Corps, Hatton Garden. The shortage of decent Liverpool accommodation limited the number of men who could be on hand at night for the first outbreak of fire. Only a maximum of eleven permanent firemen, by night, were available.

On the credit side, in his report of 1892, Nott-Bower was able to emphasise that Liverpool's fire department remained remarkably cost effective because few policemen or an average of only three per day, had to be taken away from their constabulary duties, to act as auxiliary firemen. The loss in a force as large as that of Liverpool's he believed was hardly noticeable.

To see how the Liverpool Fire Brigade's operational

efficiency compared with other major fire brigades Nott-Bower contacted the head constables, or chief fire officers, of the ten largest towns in England. In his report he enclosed the following table to summarise the strength, the composition and the cost of each.

Town	Number of Firemen employed soley on Fire Brigade Duty				Number of Firemen who performed (more or less) Police duty	Gross cost of Fire Brigade during last completed year (1891)
	Super-intendent	Deputy Super-nt	Engineer	Firemen		
						£ s. d.
Glasgow	1	3	–	98	–	14,310. 0. 0.
Liverpool	1	2	4	19	260	5,546. 8. 3.
Manchester	1	1	6	75	–	11,654. 5. 10.
Birmingham	1	1	7	50	–	8,100. 0. 0.
Leeds	1	–	–	6	37	No Information
Sheffield	1	1	2	–	18	1,145. 13. 1.
Edinburgh	1	2	2	41	–	4,086. 14. 1.
Bristol	1	–	–	–	The whole police force	No Information
Bradford	1	1	2	1	**	1,784. 9. 1.
Nottingham	1	1	3	1	19	1,732. 0. 0.
Hull	–	–	–	–	23	1,463. 6. 6.
Salford	1	–	3	17	–	4,561. 18. 3.
Newcastle	1	1	–	7	33	2,149. 10. 3.

*It must not be forgotten, in comparing the number of men, employed solely as firemen in LIVERPOOL, with the figures given for other towns, that grooms and drivers as well as watermen, are not included in the Liverpool strength (inasmuch as they are members of the Mounted Police, and of the Water Department respectively), whereas in most other towns they are INCLUDED in the strength of the firemen given above.

**In Bradford supplementary firemen are obtained by employing tradesmen and artisans residing in the vicinity of the Fire Station, who follow their ordinary avocations, but are paid for time spent attending fires, or at fire drill. In cases of urgency Police Constables are also employed.

It will be seen from the above table that a majority of towns – Glasgow, Manchester, Birmingham, Edinburgh and Salford – had, in addition to Metropolitan London, adopted a fire brigade wholly independent, or nearly so, of the respective police forces. The majority, which included Liverpool, Leeds, Sheffield, Bristol, Bradford, Nottingham, Hull and Newcastle, had in common with most other large towns, the police fire brigade system. It was also obvious that the latter system worked at a considerably smaller cost than the former.

Liverpool had to employ a particularly large number of auxiliary firemen to safeguard the immense quantities of cotton stored in the city. With the cotton packed into closely grouped warehouses, these buildings were the city's greatest fire risk and necessitated additional stringent security.

Any independent fire brigade establishment in Liverpool, Nott-Bower was convinced, would have had to be made much stronger, in proportion to the area and the population safeguarded, than those of Glasgow, Manchester and the other major towns in the table. Liverpool's most valuable property was of an entirely different character compared to that of others.

After a lengthy enquiry he estimated that only 120 to 130 full-time men organised into an independent brigade could protect the seaport at a level equal to the existing standards. He was totally supported by James Willis who had previously been in charge of the Salford Fire Brigade. On the basis of his experience he was able to estimate that a separate system would have cost about £17,500 per annum, or about fifty per cent more than the current police fire department.

Finally, one other question of vital importance which he examined was the effectiveness of communicating the fire alarm by telephone. Two modes were available; there were phones in the twenty four police and fire stations distributed throughout the town and the docks; and there were those 210 private telephones placed at the disposal of the police. The general effectiveness of telephonic communication was shown by the fact that of the 317 fires occurring in 1892, no fewer than 155 were extinguished within a quarter of an hour of the alarm being given; 65 within half an hour; 53 within an hour; 19 within two hours; 10 within three hours; whilst only 15 took over three hours.

The development of the brigade, until Nott-Bower's resignation in 1902, benefited from being splendidly organized but was handicapped by a shortage of suitable stations. When the city boundaries were extended in 1895, the brigade was not able to take over the area formerly protected by the Walton Local Board because there was no suitable station in the district. Even when the north district station at Westminster Road, was completed, in the latter year, the Bootle Fire Brigade continued to serve the Walton district until 1898.

Nott-Bower, believing that better facilities might be more speedily gained from increased funding, had again raised the thorny problem of the fire insurance offices' contribution, in 1895. He felt it was reasonable to do so because in the previous year they had contributed only £1,000 to the total expenditure of £10,000. By 1897 the companies still refused to increase their contributions even though total expenditure had risen to £15,000.

By the end of his period of office, the brigade was still the most respected on Merseyside. In the magazine The Fire Call, November 1900, it was described as a Model Police Brigade, with the "envied reputation of having one of the best equipped and organised brigades". It is not surprising therefore to find that in Nott-Bower's period of office, official enquiries as to its operation were received from as far afield as Budapest, from the chief of police 1890 and St. Petersburg, from the president of the Imperial Russian Technical Society, in November 1891. By 1898 there was a full-time staff in Liverpool of 50 manning appliances at six main fire stations. Auxiliary firemen manned some 24 Fire police stations.

Liverpool's self reliance in fire control owed much to the

willingness of its wealthy merchants, traders and other businessmen to agitate for sufficient resources for the fire department to efficiently fight fires. Once they had decided upon the location and the scale of a fire the constables could use the Siemen's police and fire signal boxes, or the private telephones, to summon an array of quite remarkable equipment. This included the steam engines, vertical pattern street escape ladders, water tower monitor wagons, horse-drawn chemical engines and the steam-powered light and air engine. The latter was adapted by the Brigade workshop engineers from a Merryweather steamer which formerly belonged to the West Derby Volunteer Fire Brigade. This facilitated the first use of smoke helmets and hand lamps for the men. The traditional dependence on beer refreshments, was meanwhile, being phased out by encouraging the ingenious incorporation of tea-making boxes on some of the fire engines. Constructed by blacksmiths, the boxes carried dry tea, tinned milk, ships biscuits and mugs.

What new advances could the men expect in the twentieth century? In 1899 a new Hatton Garden headquarters was finally opened and in the same year the workshop engineers there converted all their steamers to oilfuel use. There was always those who were keen to try out such innovations but the dependable traditional equipment, like the horse-drawn hose and reel carts, still had deep rooted support. The brigade's horses were greatly admired by the public and kept with pride and affection by those stables crews who felt horses were the only reliable means of hauling the fire appliances into the suburban districts. In contrast to the care lavished on these magnificent animals the lot of many ordinary firemen remained painfully austere.

Chapter Six

A Fireman knows no rest

Citizens throughout the Merseyside district became accustomed by the end of the nineteenth century to look upon their policemen – including the fire auxiliary constables – as being constantly on call to deal with a whole range of problems. Whilst their borough policemen might truly be regarded as jacks of all trades – often acting as firemen, ambulance drivers, police patrol wagon drivers and as mounted policemen – many regarded themselves as 'municipal slaves'.

In Liverpool their plight was aptly summarised in some of the popular Victorian verse of the era, which included The Lament of the Bold Street Policeman. In this the constable declared "I walk my rounds on Sunday good – a bobby knows no rest – And have to watch my fellowmen go out in best suit dressed".

As auxiliary firemen these constables endured the harshest of working conditions. Though they enjoyed secure employment the 'continuous system' of work permitted them only 24 hours leave every 14 days. Some of them had mid leave but by tradition firemen were looked on as being similar to domestic servants. They were never allowed out for any length of time in case they might be needed.

Within the ranks of the North West's firemen there were those who despised the continuous system of duty. Opponents of the system felt it made the fireman's life miserable as they became "sick and tired of seeing one another's faces" and had to listen to "the same old tales day in and day out". Many believed they should be allowed to get away from their station and enjoy a better social life.

Other colleagues argued against them particularly where there was a shortage of local housing. These felt that with growing families they were better off staying at the fire stations. Most of those it would appear had communal washhouses with mangles and sinks for wives to come in to them to do their washing.

Few firemen supporters of either argument felt satisfied with the spartan conditions to be endured whilst travelling on their engines. Most still journeyed to a fire by standing on the outside 'box' and holding on by a handrail. Such exposed appliances, especially at high speed were dangerous. Crew members were often forced to dress en route to a fire. Injuries and fatalities occurred as some men tumbled off at street corners. Others continued to suffer serious illnesses by being soaked at a fire and having to return to their base in vicious weather on a cold winters night. Few could feel satisfied in this era with the differing superannuation arrangements across the region.

Facing such adversities, a majority still manifested the British bulldog breed qualities with which they were associated. Local borough brigades were generally composed of tough, dedicated and well-drilled individuals. As danger approached they stayed at their posts until ordered to withdraw or until they collapsed.

Even within the more professional borough brigades firemen sensed that basic improvements were vital to improve their well-being and their operational efficiency. As a direct consequence of their enforced subservience there grew a strong movement of intensely frustrated firefighters. These sympathised with the widespread pattern of labour unrest and this disaffection rose to the surface in the volatile transport strikes of 1911 in Liverpool.

The common ideals of better wages and a shorter working

week inevitably appealed to those trades union enthusiasts within the firemen's ranks. The Liverpool seamen and railway workers who went on strike in the summer of that year showed the gathering momentum of feelings and matters in the port came to a head on Bloody Sunday, August 13th.

Outside the larger boroughs, full-time firemen continued to be few in numbers compared to the risks they might face. Such risks continued to increase for them, nevertheless, as on an evergrowing scale Merseyside's industrial processes became increasingly more complex. Liverpool, Birkenhead, Southport and St. Helens developed technical innovations which meant that their firefighters required improved fundamental instruction in building construction techniques, chemical processes and electrical apparatus.

Those citizens living outside these boroughs were often left under small local authorities with limited resources. Some declined to ask for 'town help' if they believed the charges for borough assistance would be too expensive. Rural treasures, including many local historical houses and their antique collections were thereby placed at considerable risk. Even on those occasions when the borough brigades went beyond their boundaries there was always a chance that firemen might be fatally delayed in attacking a fire because their fire engine hose and hydrant fittings were not standardised. Liverpool Fire Brigade was an exception to these problems. When the Brigade agreed to render assistance to other local authorities, the necessary adaptors were carried on the appropriate appliances.

Delays in locating an adequate water supply became crucial, even at small fires, when there was no local source. Some of the region's brigades helped alleviate this problem by the introduction of the chemical engine in the early decades of the twentieth century. These machines mounted a large cylinder of water, carrying up to sixty gallons, on the chassis. The cylinder also housed bicarbonate of soda with a bottle of sulphuric acid. When a fireman broke the acid bottle by pressing a plunger, the chemicals mixed and made large quantities of carbonic gas driving the water at great pressure through the attached hose reel.

The earliest chemical engines failed to allow any shut-off until the water was completely used. Improved engines eventually incorporated a shut-off valve by using bottles of compressed gas that were mounted on the water container. The Merseyside town which set the example for using these horsed chemical engines was Liverpool.

The latter imported one in 1896 from Chicago, U.S.A. The machines were valued by the firemen for, firstly, providing them with a speedy first-strike jet of water that they could use to extinguish a small fire or constrain a larger one until a hydrant could be utilised. Secondly, the use of a rubber hose and an easy 'turn off' facility on the chemical engines – particularly in home or shop fires – meant water did not escape 'en route' as it did with canvas hosed appliances.

Before the First World War improvements in apparatus amongst some of the other local brigades were also introduced whenever their funding permitted it. Some of those brigades handicapped by limited financial support still only used hand pumps, and were envious of the larger borough brigades. The latter in contrast, introduced turntable fire escape ladders, converted their steamers to oilfiring fuel and even purchased the revolutionary self-propelled motorised fire engine.

Liverpool again led the way. Some of its engineers, in 1901, attempted to replace the steam engine – with its unwieldly coal carts in tow – by opting to use a motorised fire tender. The Liverpool Watch Committee decided it might use the tender if it proved to be faster and more reliable than any of their horsed appliances. Approached by the local agents for Daimlers, i.e. the Liverpool Royal Carriage Company, they approved of the company's construction of a special body on to a Daimler Chassis F.

For their part the fire brigade engineers detached a sixty gallon chemical engine from one of their vehicles and fitted it to the company's vehicle. This permitted them to carry a six man crew aboard the machine together with hose, stand-pipes and other small apparatus.

G. V. Blackstone has vividly described how one of the Carriage Company's employees, G. H. Bechtel, took charge of the Daimler tests. These had to incorporate 'surprise' turnouts in competition with some of the horse-drawn steamers. Bechtel was a diligent man and kept his machine constantly at the ready. He kept the machine 'warm' to match the prompt action of those firemen who stood at the back of each stable stall where a horse was kept for the steamers. On the first call-out to a cotton warehouse fire, he responded so rapidly that he went off without his crew.

On the final night of the test they raced out into Dale Street and across the City but before they had climbed into Hardman Street they were involved in a collision. Their policeman colleagues tried to halt the traffic but the Daimler eventually hurtled into a tram car, hitting it and 'tearing out most of its side panel'. Throughout the entire episode the motorised firemen hung on for their lives as they ran their final race.

In spite of the boldness and willingness of civic authorities to finance these prospective improvements, the machine was too unpredictable. Its open flame ignition system required constant supervision and intermittently fired whilst in operation. Liverpool's firemen had their own rude euphemism 'Farting Annie' for this characteristic. After lengthy trials the Chief Officers felt it could not be depended upon as a 'first turn-out' machine and demoted it to the role of a stores tender.

This failure reprieved the steam engines for a short time. Perhaps it was not surprising that a Merryweather Fire King, with its steam propelled 500 g.p.m. pump was purchased in 1903, for £950.00 as a first appliance. So successfully did the men operate this machine that a further five were purchased within the next three years. Trials with electric appliances were also undertaken. These included those with Simonis Braun

Magirus turntable escape, 1907-21; Simonis Braun chemical escape 1908-20; Simonis Porsche with electric hose-reel pump, 1909-20; and Braun electric general purpose tender, 1910-1919.

Nevertheless the competitive trials between the motorised and the horse-drawn appliances continued widely across the country. At the same time the increasing dependence of fire brigades on other mechanisation such as those motor pumps produced by the Dennis Brothers of Guildford, in 1908, and that of Leyland's, in 1910, meant that the much respected chemical engines were to be soon superseded. This was particularly so when Halley, Simonis and Stanley produced a turbine motor pump in 1908. Fire Brigades throughout the Merseyside region purchased these type of pumps in one form or another.

Some brigades, as in Liverpool, used their self-propelled steamers whenever possible, but by the beginning of the First World War few appeared likely to survive the growing popularity of the motorised fire engines. Birkenhead, Bootle, Liverpool and Southport all had at least one form of Dennis Pump before 1920. The early Leyland pumps, too, were known to have been adopted by Birkenhead, Bootle, Great Crosby, Liverpool, St. Helens and Wallasey.

Even when the larger brigades established schools to train motor drivers the horse-drawn steamer still refused to give way to the new motorised machines. In the rural areas steamers were retained and used in the air raid emergencies of 1940. Many firemen were reluctant to see them replaced. In the larger brigades they regarded the tradition of keeping them at the ready in their stations – with a constant gas powered flame under their boilers to maintain the water close to steam pressure – as an irreplaceable tradition. In contrast some of the smaller brigades relied on 'rapid rise' firelighters and oily rags to raise steam on the way to a fire.

The regard for the expertly trained horse was also deeply rooted. Many town dwellers for their part enjoyed the excitement of waiting to see the station doors being drawn open by the pulling of a lanyard. In some of the engine houses such as that in the heart of Bootle, bemused spectators would gather to witness the use of 'the swinging harness'. In such an operation horses would be made to trot out of their stables to position themselves by poles. Lines attached to toggles would remove their rugs and the harness hanging by pulleys from the engine house ceiling would then be lowered onto their backs. When the harness incorporated split collars and spring clips they could be clasped around their necks and have their fire engines racing away within minutes.

A further vital development on Merseyside, too, was the increasing dangers posed by the manufacture of the new plastics. Firemen grew to recognise that celluloid was perhaps the greatest problem in most homes because it could ignite from the heat of the fire. The use of toys, combs, beads, brooches and even men's collars throughout the region became a constant threat. Within the boroughs and small townships the popularity of the new cinematographs probably posed the most common threat to large gatherings of people.

The impact of the popularity of petroleum for the motor vehicle was increasingly felt. The spread of petrol pumps brought a fresh danger into both the urban and rural districts and forced the brigades to search for new safety guidelines. It was openly acknowledged that the use of water was too dangerous at a petrol fire and it became necessary for firemen to smother the flames by means of an inert gas or by use of foam compounds that excluded oxygen. This also spurred many firemen to improve their own level of education and many looked to join professional associations to help promote their interests. Chief Officer J. T. Burns of Birkenhead 1907-33, was a founder member of the Institute of Fire Engineers and became President of the Professional Fire Brigades Association. He also encouraged his men to become members of the Fire Brigades Union as soon as it was formed.

Whereas Liverpool, in the mid-Victorian era, had implemented local bye-laws for the storage of petrol, other localities were less fortunate. They were afforded limited cover by the Act for the Safekeeping of Petroleum, 1862 and the amendments of 1868, '71 and '79. Such legislation was essentially limited to the use of paraffin oil in domestic lamps and the potentially disastrous lower flash point of petrol, as used by the motor vehicle, was not widely safeguarded in law. For many local citizens the danger was to persist until as late as 1926 when effective laws for the storage of petrol were finally entered on the statute books.

The development of the petrol engine for fire pumps radically improved immediately prior to the outbreak of the First World War. Several local authorities still clung to their traditional use of their steamers. They were evident on Merseyside as two well-known municipal buildings suffered serious fire damage. In 1912 when the town hall in St. Helens was threatened a Shand Mason steamer was put into action. The following year a Birkdale urban district fire crew attended with their steamer at the Southport market hall, in King Street.

Fires in municipal public buildings sharply focused the attention of their local close-knit communities upon the ability of their local firefighters to protect them. This was heightened during the First World War, 1914-18. Though London and the Eastern Counties received by far the greatest damage from the fire-raising weapons of the German aerial attacks, the North-Western fire brigades did not escape from some of the most dramatic consequences of the war.

When the threat of aerial attacks was brought home by Zeppelins dropping bombs in the north-east on Wallsend, Hebburn and Blyth it became obvious that there were no strategies for the co-ordination of resources in areas such as Merseyside. Brigades were also heavily depleted by the recall of reservists from their ranks to the British armed forces. Conscription, in 1916, prompted by the mounting casualties on the Western Front, brought exemption for the professional firemen but not those who acted as retained or volunteer firefighters. Newton-le-Willows and Prescot are known to have had retained brigades, whilst those with volunteers included, Formby, Birkdale, Great Crosby, Hightown, Hoylake and West Kirby, Huyton-with-Roby and Maghull. A further depletion of resources within the brigades was also felt as the insatiable demands by the army for horses caused a shortage of those needed to haul the steamers.

These demands sometimes drew the local brigades into schemes of mutual co-operation. In 1915 Liverpool agreed to help several of its neighbouring rural brigades. The Huyton-with-Roby Urban District Council was particularly grateful at this time for it only had hand appliances at its disposal. Whiston Rural District Council, separate from the Parish of Whiston itself, which had the help of the Prescot Brigade, was also covered by the Liverpool men. In turn Liverpool also agreed to attend all the calls for help from the Earl of Derby at Knowsley Hall and Earl of Sefton, at Croxteth Hall. They practically stood at the ready with an appliance when members of the Royal Family resided at the latter during the Aintree race course season.

In general terms Merseyside's fire outbreaks during the Great War never got out of hand. Only a small number of incendiary bombs were dropped, preponderantly in the South-West of England and the bombs were scattered over a wide area. The greater toll for the north came from those casualties incurred in the fires at the temporary munitions' factories in the region. The great demand for high-explosive artillery shells, for the Western Front, had precipitated the risk-taking which accompanied the lack of safety regulations. Explosives and fires frequently occurred as a result and that at Morecambe, October 2nd 1917, was a regional disaster for the north-west.

Such incidents were often obscured at the time and were not reported in local newspapers due to strict censorship. This inevitably prevented many citizens from realising that there was a total lack of liaison between many local forces. Liverpool's superintendent, George Oakes, accompanied a firecrew and pump which travelled 60 miles to the scene of the explosion. This happened at the White Lund national shell filling factory in the Lancashire seaside resort. Those brigades refusing to attend echoed the long-standing excuse that it was "not within their area" and they were not obliged to do so.

Though the incident, which lasted several days, had begun with a small fire, ten firemen were killed in the first explosion. In total the eventual conflagration damaged 250 acres of the 400 acre site. Firemen joining the Liverpool helpers came with their pumps from Preston, Lancaster, Blackpool, Barrow-in-Furness, Chorley, Leyland, Fulwood and Horwich. With no one officer in overall command, the attempts to control operations collapsed in chaos. Those who did attend received grateful recognition from Central Government. Liverpool's representatives were sent a letter of thanks from the Home Secretary, Winston Churchill, for taking part in the tremendous efforts to contain the fire.

The Great War acted as a catalyst. It exposed the need for greater regional unity and co-operation between neighbouring fire brigades to meet national emergencies. It also induced more firemen to realize they had common, fundamental grievances. After 1918 a wave of strikes and industrial action across Britain was supported by pockets of discontented firemen, especially in London. The eyes of many provincial colleagues focused upon these as they formed their London Fire Brigade Representative Body. Soon after, when a brigade union was formed to encompass the whole country, its largest unit was the London FBRB.

As union activity spread across the entire country, the new body went quickly to work to secure notable improvements. These included one day's leave in every ten, a rise of five shillings, or 25 pence, per week in addition to the war bonus and the government's announcement that it intended to establish a commission to review the hours of work, the wages and the pensions of firemen throughout the United Kingdom.

Chapter Seven

Between the Wars,
1918 to 1939

Between the two World Wars, from 1918 to 1939, Merseyside's fire brigades generally followed the pattern that evolved in other areas within the United Kingdom. The region's fire service remained a fragmented one. Many of the rural districts outside the boroughs still lacked adequate resources for fighting large fires and there was no system for the standardisation of appliances and apparatus. Some of the rural areas had become so bereft of resources, after the Great War, that they were left without horses, or traction, for their steamers and were unable to stage even a small 'turnout'. Attempts to tow steamers with motor cars invited accidents on steep hills as the brakemen struggled with their manual controls. The working conditions for many also left much to be desired.

The post Great War years continued to be difficult for those firemen seeking to improve such conditions through trades union representations. In London the County Council had flatly refused to recognise the firemen's chosen union during the War. Some 2000 had joined a branch of the National Union of Corporation Workers. In the provinces most of the professional firemen joined either this branch or the Municipal and General Workers' Union.

Large numbers of police firemen sought union representation through the Police and Prison Officers' Union. The extremists in this union demanded redress of their two long-standing grievances. Their first which had festered throughout the war years, had been the denial of their 'right to confer'. Their second embittered complaint was the failure of police pay to rise with the cost of living. When they contrasted their meagre weekly wages with those of the munitions workers many had felt bitterly aggrieved.

Immediately after the First World War the fall in trade and the growth in nationwide unemployment encouraged a government drive for economy. In the face of its long term gestures of reconciliation a wave of strikes spread across the country and heralded more. A distinct change in the country's trade unions' attitude was notable after mid 1919.

On Merseyside matters reached a head in Liverpool, Birkenhead and Bootle. With the coal miners strike still not settled the fever of unrest broke out on both sides of the River Mersey and in other British ports. Pockets of professional firemen were as restive as other sections of the working population. Revolution was feared as police representatives from Liverpool, Birkenhead, Bootle and Wallasey – joining those from three other forces, Metropolitan, City of London, and Birmingham – went on strike, 31st July 1919. Their branch of the National Union of Police and Prison Officers, with many ex-servicemen amongst them, chose to risk their jobs and pension to protect their union's existence. Formal recognition of the latter had been refused by the Home Secretary.

The stunning impasse between the Liverpool Watch Committee and 954 members of the force led to troops and tanks on the streets, destroyers and a battleship on the river, as looters emerged in both Liverpool and Birkenhead. Those police who did strike suffered irrevocably. After being dismissed they were refused reinstatement and forfeited their pension rights. When widespread labour unrest continued in this difficult post war period, alternative sources of unemployment became scarce.

In a race against time, starting on March 1st of that year the Government had appointed a committee under

Lord Desborough to review police pay and conditions. With the Home Secretary undertaking, in May, to accept recommendations to improve pay and to set up alternative representative machinery – embodied in the Police Federation – the prospects of total police strike support were completely undermined. After the first twenty four hours the police strike collapsed.

Promises of help from other unions were not fulfilled. The main body of the professional firemen, in the big towns particularly, were left to reflect on the lack of uniformity between their pay scales and the retention of the contentious continuous duty system. With the Professional Fire Brigades Association pressing for the two-shift system, one Merseyside fire department became noteworthy for a remarkable short-term achievement. Birkenhead became the first to adopt the system. In February 1919, firemen auxiliaries in the borough went on two twelve hour duty shifts, with an 8 shillings higher rate of pay than the ordinary constables. By 1922 in the face of economic restraints, the brigade had reverted to continuous duty. Elsewhere there was less success and the system remained as standard in most provincial fire brigades until 1941.

Progress towards providing an effective country-wide fire service remained totally disjointed until the Second World War revealed national inadequacies on an alarming scale. Even after the fine recommendations of the Royal Commission of 1921 there remained some industrialised county boroughs very poorly protected and some country districts even worse.

Fortunately for the men, four years later the Fire Brigade Pensions Act became a milestone and did much to improve the status of those in the fire service. With the General Strike, in 1926, highlighting the desperation of some 2,500,000, unemployed, the firemen appeared to be in an enviable position but this lessened their chances of improved conditions of service for several decades. It was only when the resurgence of Germany stirred Britain from her apathy that out of necessity the British fire service had to be reformed.

Meanwhile, many borough fire officers sought every opportunity to improve their own technical competence and those volunteers in the rural districts were keen to learn from them. Liverpool's men, for example, sought to undertake examinations in mechanics, hydraulics, electricity, chemistry and building construction. Those employees of the Watts family of Speke Hall – then outside the city boundaries – sought to use the expertise of the Liverpool men. In 1915 they reached an agreement to be regularly drilled by them on their estate, particularly in the operation of the Shand Mason horse-drawn steamer.

Once again the attention of the members of the borough brigades of Liverpool, Birkenhead, Southport and St. Helens was focused on two principal developments. Firstly the boroughs were intent on dealing efficiently with the most dangerous fires that occurred within their boundaries. Secondly they were concerned to improve their own conditions of service.

Although it is impossible to record in detail each local major fire some of the most notable are vividly captured in the photographic archives of the various Merseyside brigades. A principal concern for all firemen between the Wars continued to be the widespread use of celluloid in the urban conurbations. Liverpool however had taken exceptional precautions to guard against the haphazard storage of cinema film. Like London and Glasgow, the seaport encouraged fire-resistant storage, ventilated compartments with several means of escape, special safety lighting and the prohibition of smoking. The Celluloid and Cinematograph Film Bill passed in 1922 helped improve matters but there were serious fires involving cinema furnishings, such as that in Newton-le-Willows in 1938.

Inter war major fires in Birkenhead included the outbreaks in 1920, at the Grange Road shopping precinct and that at the coach works in the same road, in 1937. Heavily industrialised

Bootle also experienced many outbreaks, these included the 1933 cotton warehouses blaze in Globe Road, and in 1934 the Hawthorne Road rubber works blaze.

Liverpool firemen had the largest number of turn outs and some of the most remarkable. In the city centre districts they included fires, such as that at the Adelphi Theatre in 1921. Among the other city fires – within the commercial and industrial districts – were included that in 1927 at the White Star Shipping Offices in James Street. At this, two firemen, Hague and Newby, were heroically led by their superior, Inspector Buckley, to rescue a trapped caretaker, his wife and their daughter from their attic home, over 100 feet above the pavement.

The modern era of industrial development also became remarkable for the emergence of new, more complex forms of fire outbreaks. In the same year as the shipping office fire an oil tanker, the Seminole, which was bound for Dingle, broke her back on the Mersey's Pluckington Bank. When some 8,000 tons of high octane petroleum spilled into the river, Liverpool and Birkenhead brigades had to "stand by". A combined police operation, enforced on all vessels the "no smoking" rule – even on the ferryboats – until the tides and winds had helped to remove the unprecedented dangers.

During the 1930s, the heroism of the firemen was again irrepressible. At one incident for example on May 6th 1930, they had to deal with the effects of a terrific explosion at Bibby's Mill in Great Howard Street which killed or injured some 37 workers. Spontaneous combustion within the milling dust was believed to be the cause of ignition. Later, humidity controls were installed to avert a similar disaster. Another new threat and challenge to the expertise of the brigade came some seven years later. In this year, 1937, the city's first air crash incident occurred in Royal Street, Everton Valley. Men of the brigade had to remove the badly burned corpse of the pilot of the aeroplane.

The region's brigades had shown some commendable

co-operation with one another. A major example of this had occurred when the Irish republican supporters of Sinn Fein, in 1920, once again plotted to attract attention to their cause by acts of terrorism. On the night of 27th September, the brigades within the area had to confront no less than fourteen simultaneous fires. Within 5 minutes of 9 pm, eleven broke out in Liverpool and Bootle warehouses and three in timber yards. With the eventual assistance of men from the brigades of Birkenhead, Waterloo, Crosby, Warrington and St. Helens, Liverpool, Bootle and Preston, they restricted the damage to £960,000 worth. Preston Fire Brigade's help – a horse-drawn steamer and crew – had arrived by rail at Liverpool's Exchange Station and operated for several days from the Hatton Garden headquarters.

Evidence of the use of paraffin cans and oil soaked rags and bolt-cutting equipment gave an indication of the sinister intent behind the fires. Six months later, the expertise of the brigades in containing fires in the rural districts was shown as some thirteen farm fires around Ormskirk and Crosby were dealt with. These outbreaks were also believed to have been simultaneously started by Sinn Fein sympathisers.

By and large, however it was widely accepted, when the Riversdale Committee was appointed in 1933, that the firefighting provisions in many regions were totally inadequate. The general permissiveness, the lack of central control and the large numbers of parish operated brigades appeared completely anachronistic as Britain began to re-arm. When Hitler was appointed as Chancellor in Germany, it was soon apparent that air raid and civil defence measures could not be grafted easily onto the former 'ad hoc' arrangements.

Despite blatantly obvious inadequacies, Britain and her fire service were to be caught almost unprepared by the Munich Crisis of 1938. The Riversdale Committee had reported in 1936 and made several vital recommendations. These included the consolidation of fire brigade law into one coherent measure; that all rate payers should have free fire service available to them; that there should be a government grant dependent upon inspection, an approved training school, the standardisation of equipment; and that the police fire brigades should allow their superintendents to consult directly with their Watch Committee.

The Fire Brigades Act of 1938 was regarded as being inadequate for peace time needs. As impending war approached it threw all responsibilities onto the local authorities in a most cynical way. Yet it did allow local authorities to make the services of the fire brigade freely available to every person. In total, however, there were no fewer than 1,440 separate fire authorities in operation in England and Wales. Standard conditions of service were not introduced and the local authorities continued to conduct their own negotiations for pay, accommodation and hours of duty. Some of the rural fire bodies did act commendably and even built new stations.

Needless to say there were marked variations in local organisation – including that on Merseyside – particularly in their recruitment of members of the Auxiliary Fire Service. Some brigades appointed a commandant and officers of the A.F.S. After preliminary training these would take almost complete control of the other recruits. Some brigades controlled the A.F.S. rigidly and gave them little status. All recruits were initially provided with a cap, overalls, boots and a steel helmet; later a tunic, trousers and waterproof leggings were added. Each trainee had to attend for a total of sixty hours of evening and weekend drill. Women were among the first recruits and were later to take on control room duties and to drive motor cars. Chief Officer G. Oakes of Liverpool was appointed H.M. Inspector of Fire Brigades with a particular brief of organising the new Auxiliary Fire Service in the region, in 1939.

With local authorities organising their A.F.S. recruits according to their own ideas, some appeared noticeably worse paid, clothed and equipped than the regular firemen. Where poor accommodation was offered and uniforms other than boots, cap, helmet and dungarees were not made available some recruits left the service to seek positions elsewhere.

It is probable that the initial lull in action or The Phoney War, gave the local A.F.S. important breathing space. The first major air raid on Merseyside did not occur until 31st August 1940, a year after Germany invaded Poland. When it initially mobilised, the A.F.S. strength of some brigades increased amid chaotic conditions, by nearly ten times. With a lack of forethought given to the selection of buildings for use as auxiliary stations, some such as garages and disused factories had no provision for bedding and cooking facilities.

It was soon evident that schools, many of which became empty as children were evacuated, could be adopted as the best auxiliary stations. Their playgrounds, kitchens and ample toilet amenities were ideal for the new occupants. By November 1940, for example, Liverpool had as many as fifty auxiliary stations within the City. The headquarters was at Pioneer Building, Dale Street. Some other local authorities in contrast demanded the return of their schools before the end of the Phoney War and firemen in uniform were insulted and catcalled as the 'darts brigade', parasites or 'scroungers'.

For civil defence purposes the country was divided into a dozen regions. Each had a regional commissioner and two deputies with broad powers. Though inter fire brigade co-ordination still appeared sketchy local provisions did improve when A.F.S. stations were connected by a direct phone link to their main control centre. From the latter pumps could be mobilised and sent to the outbreaks of fire as required. Finally, in 1940 the Police and Firemen Employment Order suspended the right of firefighters to resign at will.

Chapter Eight

German Bombers over Merseyside, Blitzkrieg

If some firefighters unjustly suffered the indignity of being heckled as 'scroungers' during the 'Phoney War', the public's attitude to them was totally reversed during the German air raids. Some pump crews, wet and dirty from their heroic exertions were to be openly cheered in the streets and some cinema audiences stood to vigorously applaud the newsreels showing firemen's heroic exploits.

Their appreciation, particularly on Merseyside, stemmed mainly from their own shared nine-month ordeal – beginning 9th August – in which they experienced at first hand the bloody horrors of heavy urban bombing raids. At first, the German Air Force sought to subdue London. When this failed the war factories in Coventry became the target and were hit hard on November 14th. The next targets were those ports such as Bristol, Liverpool and Southampton which received the growing supplies of weapons, munitions, raw materials and food from the United States of America and those other countries opposed to Hitler's oppression in Europe.

Some Merseysiders initially reacted with disbelief because they felt that a bombing campaign could not happen. "They can't get over the Pennines", was a common expression. Other wiser citizens, in contrast, feared the worst. Certainly the senior fire officers had reason to do so. Before the National Service Act, April 1941, which introduced conscription, the numbers of trained and experienced firemen may have appeared to have been adequate for local needs.

These firemen were to be supplemented by the A.F.S. members and supervised by a controller in each town. Liverpool, Birkenhead and Bootle, for example, had their town clerk placed in charge. In Wallasey, it was the chief constable, in Litherland, Waterloo and Crosby the clerk to the Lancashire County Council took on the responsibility. As far as possible, mutual assistance was to be organised by the Liverpool Town Clerk who became overall group controller.

Unfortunately, though there were to be many deeds of gallantry and countless quiet acts of heroism by the civil defence personnel of Merseyside, the Home Office concluded after the May 1941 attacks that firefighting arrangements for the United Kingdom needed wholesale reorganisation. The rescue services, the wardens and women of the W.V.S. helped all those involved with firefighting, rescue work and first aid on Merseyside but at the height of the Blitz the Home Office felt it had to send additional assistance to the regional commissioner. Commander Firebrace thus arrived in Liverpool to review the need for greater cohesion between the regular firefighters and the A.F.S. throughout the area.

The Commander supported the view that the brigade workshop did not have sufficient facilities to deal with the level of repairs, the maintenance of the pumps and vehicles when subjected to continuous bombing. He further felt that communications were inefficient and the arrangements for receiving reinforcements were poor. In these circumstances the chief superintendent of the Liverpool Fire Brigade was released from his onerous duties and A. P. L. Sullivan, a London Fire Brigade superintendent arrived to take over temporary command.

It was perhaps hardly surprising that the eventual flames, craters, rubble and broken bodies scattered across Merseyside tested many to their limits of endurance. Those initially put to the test were the people of Birkenhead and Wallasey, in 1940. The first casualty was at 12.30 a.m. on 9th August when a stick of bombs had been dropped on Prenton. This was followed by another of seven high explosive bombs on Wallasey. In all there were 32 casualties in this raid as a railway embankment, houses and streets were hit.

Next, came Liverpool's first stick of bombs on the night of 17th to 18th August. Further night raids were made on Liverpool, Birkenhead and Wallasey in the same month. Liverpool's firemen had to confront over 100 fires alone – most, thankfully, being small. A number of houses, shops and offices were hit together with Liverpool's Custom House, adjacent to the Albert Dock, and across the River Mersey, Wallasey's Town Hall.

This marked the start of a trial by ordeal of three months. In September, Merseysiders experienced another twenty eight raids; fifteen in October, and then nine in November – an average of one per night. Liverpool, Birkenhead, Bootle, Wallasey and Crosby all received at least four raids each.

Local citizens in general realized that these attacks were small and relatively ineffective. The war of nerves was more intense especially at night and for those who lived near the docks. In late afternoons mothers and children had to trek to their neighbourhood air raid shelters. Fathers often joined them, after a day's work, in the search for a sound night's sleep.

During September, 1940, the raids became sharper. On the night of 21st September, Liverpool's Central Railway Station was hit and train coaches damaged. A substantial fire bomb raid on the docks and warehouses followed five nights later. Two theatres caught fire – one of these, Birkenhead's world famous Argyle was gutted.

Merseysiders' real baptism of fire occurred in the raids of 28th to 29th November when hundreds of high explosive and incendiary bombs were dropped. The main weight of attack lasted for about two and on half hours after 7.23 p.m. A public air raid shelter in the basement of Liverpool's Junior Technical School, at Durning Road, was destroyed by a direct hit, fire broke out and though some sixty persons were rescued, 180 others were killed in the incident.

It was the Christmas raids on 20th to 22nd December, each lasting more than ten hours that so completely stretched firefighting resources. Food warehouses in Dublin Street and the Waterloo Grain House fires were among the most regrettable of dock incidents. At some principal civic buildings, such as the Cunard Buildings and the Dock Board Offices at the pierhead, small fires occurred. The nearby Exchange Railway Station was closed for a time.

Both Liverpool and Bootle citizens experienced a great deal of housing damage. Those people crowded under the railway arches used as a shelter in Bentinck Street, suffered a direct hit and 42 lost their lives. The northern dock areas experienced a particularly heavy 'rain of fire' and high explosive bombs on the second night.

St. George's Hall, at the Liverpool City centre was badly damaged and many houses in the Anfield district, home of Liverpool F.C., witnessed the night's worst tragedy when a direct hit on a shelter caused 74 persons to lose their lives.

Whilst the air raids' wrath was spread across Bootle, Birkenhead, Seaforth and Wallasey, the main devastation was borne by Liverpool. In Roe Street, a fire brigade crew of seven were amazingly unhurt as their engine, responding urgently to a call, was driven into a crater. Among the buildings reported as badly damaged were the Mill Road Infirmary, the Gaiety Cinema, St. Anthony's School, Crescent Church and St. Alphonsus' Church. In total, during these three nights, 356 persons lost their lives. Wallasey alone suffered 119 of the fatalities.

Shortly after this dreadful ordeal, the Minister of Home Security appealed for volunteers to form street fire parties and he introduced compulsory civil defence duties to form the basis of the fire guards scheme. On January 15th, the Fire Precautions Business Premises Order was adopted and local authorities were among those required to make adequate provisions for the detection and combating of fires in vital business and industrial districts. Men aged 16 to 60 years had to register for part-time duty of up to 48 hours per month. Though fire watching proved uncomfortable and dangerous it was felt that the fire guards undertook much useful work, especially in the later raids.

At the beginning of 1941 the pace of the attacks slackened for a time. The next heavy attack was made in March. The main brunt of the German effort was borne by the docks, especially on the Cheshire side of the River Mersey. Birkenhead and Wallasey had reason to believe this was 'their raid', though Liverpool did not entirely escape.

In Wallasey widespread bombing gave the borough its worst experience of the war. Gas, electricity and water services were hit and more than 160 persons were killed. In Birkenhead a great number of small fires had to be dealt with and the General Hospital had to be evacuated. Whilst the Birkenhead borough had 288 fatalities in March most occurred on the 12th of that month. Liverpool in comparison lost 101 citizens in March. There were more raids before the end of April but casualties were generally light and the incendiary bombs were quickly smothered by members of the new fire guard.

Many of those fighting the fires resulting from the German's March Campaign had witnessed the arrival of firemen brought in by the regional authorities. These and other service personnel had been collected from 39 cities and towns in Lancashire, Cheshire and North Wales. One of the incoming parties – from Hoylake – was hit by a high explosive bomb and its members were either killed or severely injured.

Those boroughs beyond Merseyside's dock target areas also suffered of course. Immense damage was incurred in Wallasey in March, too, as a large proportion of private houses became uninhabitable. Some eleven churches were hit and Poulton's electricity works and gas holders were put out of action. The effect on Birkenhead was equally disastrous as many people were either killed, injured or trapped by fire. At Bebington many persons were also killed.

Again the work of restoration had to be organised. Military and home guard assistance had to be sent in from beyond Merseyside. Workers in their hundreds were mobilised as grabs, bull-dozers, cranes and other transport concentrated upon the task of restoring the local war effort.

In May came the enemy's most desperate attempt to ruin the Port of Liverpool. If the destruction of the dock system itself had been achieved, it was believed, the morale of Merseyside would have been broken. The raids were to continue for the first eight nights of the month and no other provincial city had to endure a cumulative attack of such proportions. An average of 270 bombers per night flew across Merseyside. A comparatively light attack was made on the opening night and less than one hundred incidents were registered in Liverpool. This and the adjacent borough of Bootle were to bear the greatest fury of the campaign.

On the second night the scale of enemy action almost doubled whilst the third saw the heaviest of the week with between six and seven hundred incidents in the two boroughs. A fire situation of dire seriousness also had to be confronted. Between the 3rd and the 10th of May, some 558 fire appliances were taken into the district. Eighteen firemen were killed and 180 suffered injuries.

The third and fourth nights witnessed the fire services being pushed beyond their limits. Liverpool's city centre and the northern docks faced several hundred fires requiring major pump attendance.

At 23.58 hrs on 3rd May, the Salvage Corps' Hatton Garden Headquarters received a direct hit from a delayed action high explosive bomb. This entered the roof and travelled through three floors before detonating at the rear of the Traphouse. Blasting the Chevrolet Trap across the road into the gates of the Fire Brigade H.Q. opposite it wrecked it completely. D/CSO. Major A. B. Hodgson, Supt, Harry Cooke, Svn, Howell A. Jones and the wife of Svn Allister were killed. The building was so badly damaged, it had to be demolished and the Corps hastily built a temporary Traphouse on the site of blitzed Corps' cottages in North Street. It adapted a surviving cottage as a temporary H.Q. and Control Room. These 'temporary' arrangements were to last for twenty years! The wrecked Trap was replaced by a Canadian Chevrolet chassis provided by the Home Office, on which the Corps staff built an enclosed body.

Whilst the May 4th to 6th attacks were moderate that on the 7th was unforgettable with 300 incidents within the two boroughs and extensive and serious fires in both the dock areas and Liverpool city centre. Across the River Mersey, New Brighton suffered on May 8th and the ferry steamship, Royal Daffodil II sank at her Seacombe moorings.

This was probably the worst night of all for the firefighters, as roads and water supplies were badly affected. From Bootle's Huskisson Dock to Gladstone in Seaforth the glow of the flames raging and burning in ships, warehouses and dockside sheds could be seen as far away as Bangor in North Wales. Those seeking to subdue the fires had to work under a steady fall of bombs whilst surrounded by ammunition in the quayside sheds and holds of ships awaiting transhipment to North Africa. On May 2nd, the steamship Malakand, berthed in Huskisson Dock, with 1000 tons of high explosive bombs was set alight as a partly inflated barrage balloon fell onto its No. 1 hatch and ignited. Around 3 a.m., as the heroic fire officer in charge, John Lappin, returned to scuttle the ship with the ship's master and a special tender with oxy-acetylene apparatus to cut a hole in the ship the ship exploded. Such was the force of the blast that some Bootle residents in houses adjacent to the docks were literally blown out of their beds.

The night was inevitably one with many grim and strenuous scenes both inside and outside the docks. One exceptionally heavy bomb, in Liverpool, demolished three large buildings, together with nearby houses, at the Mill Road Infirmary. Whilst dockers, nurses and helpers worked steadily to release the trapped and move out the injured, a large fire burned at a factory less than one hundred yards away as the high explosive and incendiary bombs continued to fall. Whilst 62 persons at the Mill Road incident lost their lives, 70 more were seriously injured.

Countless civilians emerged as unsung heroes at this time. An enemy bomb, for example, hit an ammunition train at Clubmoor, May 4th, and set it on fire so that wagon after wagon blew up. A number of L.M.S. railwaymen showed incredible courage as they uncoupled the rear section of the train and shunted it away before those detached wagons, laden with sea mines, could be reached by the flames.

Other citizens and particularly members of the civil defence service suffered heavy casualties. By the end of the week 28 wardens and W.V.S. were killed; 11 police and 5 rescuemen were killed and others were injured.

Those who survived were left to endure scenes of total destruction. Ruined Liverpool buildings included the Head Post Office, the Central and Bank Exchanges, the Mersey Dock Offices, the George's Dock Buildings, Oceanic Buildings, the India Buildings, the Corn Exchange, the Museum and many churches including St. Nicholas Parish Church and St. Luke's Church. The homeless persons included 51,000 in Liverpool and 23,000 in Bootle and the hardest hit inevitably were those living in the dockside neighbourhood.

May 1941 thus marked out one of the most heroic chapters for Merseyside's firefighters. Relief crews and appliances from 123 brigades came, many for their first experience of a major conflagration. The Liverpool Brigade alone lost more than 40 members between 3rd September 1939 and 17th August 1941. Other brigades, too, particularly those from Birmingham and Blackpool, suffered serious loss of life in offering assistance. Liverpool Fire Brigade and its A.F.S. members received the following awards arising from the war, viz, six George Medals, eight M.B.E., nine British Empire Medals, and eight awards of the Liverpool Shipwreck and Humane Society.

The orderliness and dignity shown by the worst affected persons was of the highest order of heroism in those catastrophic days. The end of their May week of trial by terror saw the enemy's main objective unrealised. If the May Blitz was a major part of the Battle of the Atlantic then the defensive achievements of Merseysiders, their firefighters and their civil defence services was a crucial factor in winning the final victory. The lack of one unified fire force, however, had greatly handicapped the defence of the region. The central government responded to this crisis with the formation of the National Fire Service after May 1941. Local firefighting provisions were never again to be so loosely arranged once this new service was organised.

Chapter Nine

Too Much, Too Late;
A National Fire Service,
1941-48

The government was forced to act quickly after the German air raids of 1940 had revealed the deficiencies in provincial firefighting. The Enabling Act of May 1941 involved the hasty introduction of the National Fire Service. This provision only lasted until 1948. It essentially formed a more centralised fire brigade structure to cope with any future air raids on the scale of those of May 1940.

August 18th 1941 was the appointed date for the new N.F.S. to take over from the former local authority brigades. This arrangement came much too late to alleviate the effects of the devastation suffered in those prime Luftwaffe target areas, such as Merseyside. Never again was the pattern of these air raids to be reproduced in a form intense enough to test the new Fire Service strength.

Merseyside was spared any further major punishment from the air. The last main attack on Britain occurred the following year, on London, 10th May. The Baedecker Raids – known because of their intention to ruin the ancient monument cities of Canterbury, Exeter, York, Norwich and Bath – took place between April and July 1942. The final air attacks were low level ones known as the Tip and Run Raids, lasting from early 1942 to almost the end of the war.

Mostly aimed at coastal towns, the latter assaults lacked the vehemence and fire dangers of those of the May Blitz.

Finally, the Little Blitz, which lasted from January to March 1944, and did not focus upon Merseyside, was principally aimed at London, with Hull, Bristol and Weston-Super-Mare as secondary targets. The full impact of the National Fire Service by 1941 was felt throughout the United Kingdom. It laid the foundations for modes of standardisation that had been undreamt of previously. With regard to the defence of the British Isles from aerial bombardment however, it was clearly a case of too much being introduced too late.

In effect some 1,600 fire brigades were reorganised by the Home Office to fit into thirty nine areas. Thirty three were in England and Wales and six in Scotland. In charge of each was a Fire Commander. Two, three or four of these commanders were to be answerable to local regional commissioners.

Attempts to move the headquarters of these commissioners to sites outside the bombing target areas were often frustrating. The most suitably situated premises had in general been taken over by the military authorities before the fire service planners had their chance to choose a new base. There was evidence of some sound forward looking planning on Merseyside. Liverpool, as early as 1939, had set up a duplicate brigade control room at Allerton, well beyond the city centre. Still later, its main headquarters was transferred from the city centre, Hatton Garden, to suburban Holly Mount in Mill Lane, West Derby.

Such measures were of further benefit when Liverpool was chosen as the headquarters of the 26th Fire Force. Consisting of eleven divisions and a fireboat section, the Force's territory extended from Southport to Crewe and included a large section of Cheshire and south-west Lancashire.

Its county boroughs included those of Birkenhead, Wallasey, Chester, St. Helens, Warrington and Southport. Four of the divisions and the largest section of the river service which at its peak numbered some 20 vessels, were centred at Liverpool.

The overall size of the Fire Force was reduced soon after the War but Liverpool retained its position as the centre of the most important and most heavily protected area in the provinces. In 1945 it received a zoning grade of 'A' from the Home Office. This was the highest grade for fire risk in the country. Herein lay the chief reason for the seaport being maintained as the strategic centre of its local regional fire service. This was to be a crucial factor in the eventual formation of the Merseyside Fire Brigade some thirty years later.

Many other provincial regions, from 1941 onwards followed in a similar pattern. These also had essentially established their wartime headquarters in requisitioned mansions in the rural outskirts beyond their built-up city centres. Inside their newly acquired large houses they built reinforced control rooms. In turn these were placed in direct communication with each of their district 'fire' stations. An essential piece of this jigsaw was added by linking the headquarters with regional H.Q. and with the London Home Office Control Room. Brigade standardisation did not end with communication procedures, however, for other vital aspects extended to pay, uniform, training, equipment, and the compilation of statistics.

From 1941 to 1947, payment of firemen, for all ranks up to divisional officer, became structured. Uniforms and rank markings for the first time became more easily identifiable across Merseyside and elsewhere. Whilst officers were expected to wear a dark blue "undress" uniform, those below the rank of a company officer had to wear a fire tunic on all duty occasions.

Both the regular and A.F.S. officers were graded and placed in order of merit. Once the selections for the senior posts had been acted upon, the regional commissioners instructed the members of the regional boards to select the divisional officers and column officers. In return the fire force commanders appointed the company officers, section leaders and leading firemen. Five grades of women officers, too, ranging from senior area officer to leading firewoman were also introduced.

A further urgent requirement, highlighted by the May Blitz

and the introduction of the N.F.S., was the need to standardise both the training and the equipment of all firefighters. With the nationalisation of the fire service the training of both officers and recruits was particularly made a matter of paramount importance. The highest grade of officers were encouraged to attend the National Fire Service College, at Saltdean, Sussex. This was supported by training for instructors, junior officers and new recruits in no less than seventy two regional and fire force training schools. For the first time a standard pattern of instruction emerged and was supported by the general availability of the National Fire Service Drill Book. Across Merseyside and the other main regions common drills for handling every piece of firefighting apparatus was precisely set out. This was a mid twentieth century innovation that was never to be superseded. The ideal of systematic training, set by several of the Victorian 'model' borough fire brigades now became a countrywide requirement.

By late 1941 the Home Office and the Scottish Office were able to issue identical orders to the twelve regional fire officers – partly in the form of the published National Fire Services instructions. This centralisation was pushed further by the Home Office's regular use of inspectors who were to arrive unannounced, at local fire brigade quarters to inspect and report upon personnel, records, stations and appliances. This form of inspection had been used for police forces since 1856.

A further step forward was the standardisation of hours of duty. For firemen, leading firemen and for section leaders the system of forty eight hours duty followed by twenty four hours leave was adopted. Company officers and those above this rank were to use the continuous duty system. Another radical development was the adoption of a common code of discipline.

Inevitably, however, there were complaints at local level against such remarkable changes. The National Fire Service continued to be placed on the alert for future heavy air raids but these were never to recur. Except for large scale practices – regarded by some senior officers as a waste of fuel – the service became dormant at a national level for lengthy periods. At the same time many basic facilities in the sub-stations were lacking. Some local authorities complained of their disappointment in the lowering of the ranks of some of their former officers and the fact that some of their own recently acquired apparatus had to be forfeited and re-distributed.

Standardisation, however, did extend to the keeping of statistics with regard to categories of fires. The supplying by the Home Office of the Manual of Firemanship fulfilled the want for an all embracing text book required by firefighters. Such progress also helped to promote the fire-preventive role of the service at a time when industry and everyday householders recognised the growing need for it.

Some notable advances came to the fore in the use of new N.F.S. equipment and machines. The evolution of the water tender from the mobile dam unit helped to overcome the shortages at the later air raid fires. Rural areas traditionally handicapped by a lack of piped supplies, particularly benefited from this. After the war this form of pump was built into the chassis of the fire engine and was no longer towed separately. This advance was to be an outstanding success in rural areas.

Merseyside's fire service arrangements were to be put to yet another test before the end of the war. When the conflict swung in favour of the Allies near the end of 1943, a concentration of munitions was built up around the ports of the south coast of England. Fire cover across this area had to be reinforced at the expense of the northern districts. For this end Operation Colour Scheme was introduced and more than ten thousand personnel both men and women and over one thousand of their pumps moved south at one week's notice. Large contingents of men and appliances were moved from Merseyside in readiness for D-Day. They were later replaced by men from Lancashire and Yorkshire with lesser domestic responsibilities.

Though many experienced officers felt, by 1944, that the N.F.S. should become permanent, it lasted only for a further three years. The Association of Municipal Corporations and other individual local authorities pressed for the return of the fire service to local control. Even though the N.F.S. had improved conditions of service and had introduced standardised hours of work, the Fire Brigades Union supported the move towards decentralisation. The Government agreed to return the service to local control – essentially to the county boroughs and the counties in England and Wales and to Glasgow and ten joint fire areas in Scotland – but it was quite determined that the previous loose approach with some six hundred authorities should not be re-introduced.

Whilst local authorities were given powers to combine to form new larger brigades, the Home Secretary could make those regulations regarding pay, hours of duty, discipline and promotions which he believed necessary. He was also empowered to oversee training standards, equipment design and performance and to set up a central Fire Service College. Those provisions regarding inspectors, a new pension scheme and the mutual assistance of neighbouring brigades at fire outbreaks close to nearby boundaries was retained. Finally, a central fire brigades advisory council was instituted to advise the Secretary of State on matters other than rank, pay, hours of work and discipline arising from the Fire Services Act 1947. Never again, it seemed would the major regions of the United Kingdom have to contend with a loosely organised and unco-ordinated local fire service.

Chapter Ten

From Fire Force
to Merseyside Brigade
1948-74

In the wave of post-war decentralisation the government's firm grip over the fire service loosened. The United Kingdom's regions regained some of their pre-war authority over their local firefighters, on 1st April 1948, when the Fire Service Bill, 1947, was enacted. On Merseyside, in effect, the 26th Fire Force was disbanded.

Though some of the smaller brigades were re-formed they struggled for many years to cope with severe post-war financial handicaps. Suitable recruits became difficult to find as the indigenous local workforce found firemen's pay and working conditions poor in relation to those of local industry. The latter being eager to restore normal production usually offered more attractive terms of employment.

Professional firefighters thereafter faced a titanic struggle to improve their working conditions and their pay. The failure of the chief officers to surmount these obstacles meant that the men in the lower ranks in particular had to undertake excessive periods of duty at a poor rate of remuneration. A basic 56 hour week had to be worked by most personnel.

Firefighters across Merseyside were to be based for much of the post-war period in outmoded stations. When the 147 United Kingdom authorities accepted responsibility for their brigades in 1948, it was hoped that it would be relatively simple for them to take on their responsibilities. In the county boroughs, firefighters soon realised that their former headquarters, workshops and district fire stations, because of wartime neglect, could not be returned to operational use without much refurbishment.

The smallest Local Authority fire brigades were not re-formed in 1948 but were replaced by the new County Fire Brigades, such as Lancashire and Cheshire. The latter had only one station problem: the stations at Heswall and Hoylake were satisfactory, but in the area around Bromborough there was no station, as the area had been covered by the Port Sunlight Fire brigade at the expense of Lever Brothers Ltd. Cheshire arranged for Port Sunlight to continue to provide this cover until a station was built at Bebington in 1959.

Elsewhere, N.F.S. temporary fire stations which were handed over were often sited for war-time needs only. Being beyond the Luftwaffe urban bombing target areas they were now too far removed from the centres of greatest peace-time risk. With manpower and materials in short supply the construction of urgently needed new stations continued as a low priority throughout the 1940s and 1950s.

Those brigades which had been traditionally well resourced had to cope with this post-war austerity, too. The re-formed City of Liverpool Fire Service, again bearing its own crest in 1948, inherited some very heavily damaged appliances. None of its own pumps had been lost and those received from the N.F.S. were gratefully accepted. It had to wait until 1950 before its first new post-war motor engine – a Dennis F7 pump with a mid-chassis 1000 g.p.m. pump – was purchased. This limousine style fire engine greatly improved the morale of crew members in this difficult era.

Liverpool's N.F.S. acquisitions also included two Esturial type fire boats, named Destiny and Esturial. These were to continue to afford protection for all parts of the River Mersey shipping area. They were to work within the mutual aid agreements which had operated across Merseyside in some form or other since the First World War.

Whilst one boat was stationed at Huskisson Dock to cover the north docks, the other operated from Queen's Number One Branch Dock for the south docks. The crews were respectively housed at the Canada Dock and Coburg Dock fire station. When a further vessel, the William Gregson, was acquired in 1949, she was fitted with modern Merryweather pumps capable of delivering 14,000 gallons per minute. This was a breathtaking advance upon Merseyside's first fire engine to be housed aboard a vessel in the Victorian era. In time the Gregson was also used as the Liverpool Port Medical Authority vessel. Its berths both at the Princes's Half Tide Dock and at the George's Landing Stage were fitted with the most modern of facilities.

Before its eventual withdrawal, after fourteen years of remarkable service, it was regarded as the finest fire boat of its type in Great Britain. At major fires on the River Mersey its presence acted as a fillip to local firemen. At one momentous fire, 9th to 11th November 1949, it assisted the two other fire boats and thirty five appliances at the disastrous Gladstone Dock conflagration. Some 800 officers and men, including some from as far afield as North Wales and Staffordshire were needed to subdue the fire.

Such co-ordinated efforts were greatly encouraged by the Home Office. After 1949 it sent inspectors annually to visit each brigade. The contingencies of the war had brought a significant awareness of the need to train all firefighters to a high national standard of technical excellence and efficiency.

As part of a rolling programme the Home Secretary sought to improve the training facilities for all personnel. As more new vehicles were acquired, a high proportion of them were fitted with two-way radio to keep their crews in touch with their control rooms. Advances in V.H.F. mobile radio apparatus had been witnessed near the end of the war. Merseyside's reliance upon fixed point warning systems, such as the Gamewell in Liverpool, were now to be gradually superseded.

In 1951 several Merseyside brigades took advantage of Liverpool's fire service training school at Speke where initial specialist instruction was offered, for example, in the use of oxy-acetylene burners. All of the region's senior officers had the opportunity to attend for tactical training at the Fire Service College, at Reigate.

Each brigade in this period was forced to confront an ever increasing spiral of specialist duties. These included a high percentage of stand-by operations on Merseyside at ships that loaded or unloaded dangerous cargoes. Increased provisions had to be made, after the 1952 Avonmouth oil installation fire, for the storage of foam compound stocks by waterfront fire brigades.

On the local domestic scene new demands were made on the fire service. These included the routine inspection of more public buildings, places of entertainment and many other classes of property. Inspection had to be made to prevent explosions or any fires of an unusual nature. Those firemen seeking training regarding the latter attended the North-West Forensic Science Laboratory where they acted in co-ordination with police and H.M. factories' electrical inspectors.

On Merseyside those adults carelessly disposing of cigarettes or those poorly supervising children – often left to play with matches – remained as high risk causes of fire outbreaks in houses.

At a national level members of the service had to take on the training and equipping of recruits to the Civil Defence and Auxiliary Fire Service as the chill of the notorious Cold War was felt across Europe. Following on from this came the prospects of nuclear warfare as atomic bombs were detonated in the U.S.A.

With the passing of the Civil Defence Bill in the same year the stark problems of rescue, casualty services and warfare on a hitherto unprecedented scale had to be faced. Some six hundred men, it was estimated, were required to form one mobile column and a large devastated city might require up to fifty columns. In this atmosphere, weekend and summer exercises were organised as part of the contingency plans.

Consequently, the A.F.S. gratefully accepted better equipment such as the new green fire engines, to work alongside the local authorities red machines. The additional appliances were particularly distinctive with their large water tenders and their lighter, built-in pumps. Across Merseyside, local firemen became familiar with the use of plastic piping, canteen vans, mobile kitchens, wireless cars, hose layers and inflatable rubber rafts as these became available in ever increasing numbers.

Many of the individual features of the pre-war brigades gradually disappeared. The grandeur of distinctive local uniforms in particular became a distant memory of a glorious past. After 1948 standard uniforms, similar to those of the N.F.S. were steadily introduced. Each local authority was permitted to insert its own special insignia on the six pointed star of its members' cap badge or on its chrome plated tunic buttons. Merseyside's firefighters generally welcomed these and the introduction, for ranks below station officer, of the open necked 'undress' uniform with collar and tie. With their introduction they were able to finally dispense with any of the remaining heavy Edwardian style fire tunics and other features such as the antiquated waist belts and tomahawk pouches.

As in the other United Kingdom provincial regions, Merseyside's firefighters had come to accept the new post-1948 ranking system. A chief officer and an assistant chief officer took charge of the larger brigades. These oversaw divisional officers, assistant divisional officers, station officers, sub-station officers and leading firemen. The smallest brigades, such as those in the urban districts, had station officers as deputy chief officers. Several war-time ranks like that of column officer disappeared.

Deep rooted grievances remained in all ranks and those concerning pay and working conditions could no longer be repressed by the beginning of the 1960s. A 'stock take' of the fire service at this time revealed much to be placed on the credit side. The post-war institutions, notably the Fire Service College, the Civil Defence Training Centre, Moreton-in-Marsh and the district training centre had settled well at their work and had consolidated the finest traditions of the service. Their unifying influence became increasingly obvious as the exchange of staff and ideas spread acceptable common standards. Equally they provoked stern challenges to practices hitherto accepted without protest. Professional firemen were expensive to train and had to be paid enough to remain in the service. The economic position of the country operated against this course as no government since the war, had felt strong enough by itself to grant substantial pay rises to public servants such as police constables and firefighters.

It was not until 1961 that the principle of introducing a 56 hour week for all operational members became accepted by the employers' representatives. Additional payments were only achieved after disputes that included refusals to carry out all but emergency work. In effect, 14th April of that year, the National Joint Council for Local Authorities' Fire Brigades finally proposed to amend the conditions of service.

The working week of operational members below the rank of station officer and assistant group officer on control room duties was reduced from a basic maximum of 56 hours in a working week to 48 hours. To implement these arrangements the establishments had to be increased. The employment of more women, initially in control rooms, was seen as one way to help introduce this increase.

These new pay arrangements appeared to dovetail well with the attempts to standardise the opportunities for promotion. When the Fire Service Appointments and Promotions Regulations came into operation, 16th May 1961, those seeking qualifications for promotion to the rank of leading fireman or sub-station officer now faced examinations made standard across the country by a central board.

For a brief period the time of uncertainty in the fire service seemed to be suspended as more up-to-date fire stations were constructed. On Merseyside these included those of St. Helens new district headquarters, Parr Stocks Road, 1959; Liverpool's Conleach Road Station, 1959, Crosby Fire Station, 1960; Birkenhead's District Fire Station, at Woodchurch, 1962, and Liverpool's Storrington Avenue, 1962.

The problem of pay, nevertheless, rumbled on as disputes in the 1960s constantly arose between employers organisations and firefighting personnel regarding this and other working conditions. The fire service, like that of the police, continued to lose its pre-war attraction. Firefighters pay sharply fell at a time when other workers commonly enjoyed security and a good pension. Firemen were also liable to work whilst others enjoyed their leisure in the evenings, at weekends and on bank holidays.

Increasing attention was also drawn to the trauma and anxieties that firefighters often endured. There was an ever growing increase in the number of malicious or false alarms. It was not unknown for some of these to result in horrific injuries to innocent bystanders and crew members as traffic congestion in town and city centres also added to the hazards of fire appliance turnouts.

New responsibilities such as the need to safeguard the handling of radioactive materials gave cause for great concern, yet stress from experiences at the fire face remained the main threat to the health of the fire officers. Many major industrial conflagrations continued to be tackled each year but those involving the deaths of, or injury to, large numbers of the public were always the most harrowing for all those involved. In time, such disasters heightened public awareness of the need to develop preventative measures whenever possible.

Home Office advice such as that in the publication, of November 1961, dealing with fire precautions in large department stores, was most welcome. This drew attention for the need to review the structure of buildings and the use of fire drills after the horrendous Hendersons' store fire in Liverpool.

In 1967 pay and hours of duty again came to the forefront of the firefighters' industrial relations. In the following year the local branches of the Fire Brigades Union and the National Association of Fire Officers came to an agreement with the employers National Joint Council for Local Authorities' Fire Brigades. The N.J.C. accepted the report of the National Board of Prices and Incomes. Increased pay was therein linked to 'higher productivity' and longer hours. In effect the average working week returned from 48 hours to 56. Inevitably it was only a question of time before this problem surfaced again.

The times, though unsettled for firemen of all ranks, continued to see trends of improvement. The older stations were still being replaced on Merseyside. Smaller peripherally sited ones became more desirable than the old town centred ones. The urban spread, combined with new restrictive building features, such as the erection of multi-storey dwellings and elevated road traffic flyovers had posed serious problems of access for pump crews, when accidents occurred. Traffic congestion at peak periods, the double parking of vehicles in narrow congested streets and vehicles being parked over hydrant box lids became the bane of fire engine drivers. Crew members had to manhandle obstructive vehicles to prevent an increase in 'burning time'. In some boroughs the Victorian steam engines were on record as attending more quickly than their modern replacements. To offset such difficulties in Liverpool the Hatton Garden Station was replaced in 1969 by new stations at Canning Place, Bankhall and West Derby Road.

As the Central Fire Service Advisory Council encouraged all brigades to improve their facilities, the staff and fire prevention sections at each brigade headquarters were significantly increased as new training posts were created. More purpose built new training centres, such as Liverpool's Storrington Avenue Station, in 1967 were brought into use. Such premises allowed for the simulation of fire incidents in a variety of differently constructed buildings each with its own obstacle course.

These exercises also encouraged the acquisition of the most modern of technological aids as they became available. Some of the most notable included the Dennis Brothers F24 multi-purpose appliance. Each model was fitted with a 400 gal. tank, foam spray equipment and was capable of bringing many types of fire under control without the need to locate and use a hydrant. Supplementing the traditional pump escape came the revolutionary Snorkel with its hydraulically powered platform. An even more refined appliance, the Tele Simonitor, Model TS M15 was brought into commission in Liverpool in November 1971. Its facilities incorporated a chassis mounted 300 gallon tank, high powered foam and water jets and its hand controlled hydraulically operated telescopic boom.

By the 1970s Merseyside's Brigade control room had also been refurbished with more modern automatic equipment. Some stations in Liverpool were eventually connected to the city engineer's transport computer to develop the use of 'green wave' routes. By these, fire appliances could proceed through one way traffic systems without being delayed by traffic lights. In 1971 in Liverpool for example, both photo-electric and ultrasonic devices were used to signal to the transport computer as soon as an appliance left a station.

By this decade, too, many watch rooms no longer needed round-the-clock manning. The watch room desks at district fire stations were replaced as miniature control panels, with multi-tone signals, and became capable of receiving and transmitting directly into loud speaker systems. At most modern fire stations the use of keymaster digital phones permitted better internal communication. The era of firemen dashing about and shouting vital messages to their colleagues had come to an end. By means of GPO priority lines, Brigade Control could operate tannoy voice alarm systems, open fire station doors, switch lights on or off and operate security locks. All such improvements in the operational efficiency of each station became vital as firefighters, by 1970s had to cope with their responsibilities under volumes of parliamentary legislation. Their statutory inspections had expanded under the following; the Factories Act 1961; the Offices, Shops and Railway Premises Act 1963; the Licensing Act 1964; the Consumer Protection Act 1961; the Theatres Act 1968; the Children's Act 1948; the Pet Animals Act 1951; the Animal Boarding Establishments Act; the Nursing Homes Act 1963; the Riding Establishments Act; the Gaming Act 1968; and the Fire Precautions Act 1971.

In addition they increased their 'goodwill inspections' to include schools, local government premises, hospitals and to the premises of the electricity boards, the gas boards, British Rail and the civic and industrial buildings. By this time they were affecting a greater number of rescues and special services than ever before. The former included those at houses, shops, clubs, public houses, multi-occupied flats and derelict houses. The special services included those involving aircraft, trapped persons, the swilling away of petrol, attending to trapped animals, unexploded bombs and even the removal of some foreign objects from members of the public.

Some duties that caused particular anxiety to the brigades were inherited from the Victorian era. These tasks were the inspectorial and enforcement obligations which, under previous petroleum and explosives Acts were transferred to them from the Weights and Measures departments, 1st October 1966. These responsibilities stemmed from the Petroleum, Regulations Acts 1928 and 1936 and the Explosives Acts 1875 and 1928.

All fire prevention officers of the rank of sub-officer and above were authorised to act as petroleum officers. District teams of these embarked upon a programme of periodic visits to all premises licensed for the storage of petroleum spirit or registered for the keeping of explosives. From 1st August 1968 these duties were extended when certain provisions of the Petroleum Consolidation Act 1928, were applied to a wide range of inflammable substances by the Petroleum, Inflammable, Liquid Order 1968. Shortly after, new provisions regarding the conveyance by road of such liquids were introduced. They included conditions affecting the installation of all service pumps.

Most importantly, emphasis was increasingly laid upon the need for fire brigades to plan in advance to cope with large-scale emergencies. The increasing growth of oil tankers in the River Mersey, the implications of larger aircraft using local airports, the danger of faster rail services and the larger numbers of people present in stores, factories and some dwelling places, were all examined. In consequence the fire brigades, police and ambulance services and local businesses were asked to produce joint disaster plans. Exercises were then undertaken in which they were able to concentrate their combined resources.

Efficient inter-brigade co-operation thus remained as the essential ingredient in the development of protective measures for the civilians of Merseyside. One outstanding example of this was the Abnormal Tanker Plan agreed to in 1972. By this the six brigades that protected the tidal reaches of the River Mersey planned, under Liverpool's leadership, to combine their resources. Each brigade was to supply equipment and appliances at designated embarkation points on the river.

Any ship within the Mersey Pilotage Area was to receive the assistance it required from any of the brigades whose territory formed part of the coastline. When required, fire crews and their equipment were to be transported by local tugs or by R.A.F. helicopters operating from Valley in North Wales. Similar inter-brigade plans were prepared for any serious incident occurring at Liverpool's Speke Airport.

When local government re-organisation in 1974, called for a reduction in the number of small provincial fire brigades, Merseyside already had a well developed framework of regional co-operation upon which to base its new fire brigade. The Brigade was to be essentially constructed upon the foundations of local firefighting evolvement as outlined above. It was now set to consolidate the finest elements of its provincial fire service history.

Chapter Eleven

The Merseyside Fire Brigade

When Merseysiders nostalgically witnessed the final 'turn outs' of their local fire brigades, in 1974, another chapter in provincial firefighting history had come to an end. The new Merseyside Fire Brigade replaced the smaller ones, 1st April of that year, and the Metropolitan County was inaugurated. The new fire service was formed by the amalgamation of the former county borough brigades of Liverpool, Birkenhead, Bootle, St. Helens, Southport and Wallasey. To these, with extra additional personnel, were added three stations from Cheshire County Brigade and seven from Lancashire County Brigade. In total this made thirty four stations. Frank Taylor, C.B.E., Q.F.S.M. who had so admirably led the Liverpool Fire Brigade, since 1962, retained his position as chief fire officer when he took charge of the Merseyside Fire Brigade. When he retired in 1976, he was succeeded by Sydney Rankin, 1976-83, Dennis I. Wilmott 1983-88 and acting Chief Officer Brian Jones, 1987-89.

Those citizens who did object to the loss of their own local fire brigade – by its absorption into a larger unit – made their objections in the face of a deeply rooted historical evolvement. This process had initially begun with pleas for help, in the Victorian era, from those lacking the protection provided by brigades such as that in Liverpool. The foundations for the latter to act as a regional headquarters for Merseyside had been emphatically laid as Liverpool's brigade answered repeated calls for assistance from beyond its boundaries before the First World War.

If the Great War emphasised the deficiencies of a loosely knit and poorly resourced federation of adjacent fire brigades then the Second World War unequivocally demanded the formation of a rigorously trained, highly mobile and well-equipped regional force.

The recurring problems arising from the frequent shortages of eligible recruits, inadequate pay and difficult working conditions continued to handicap the ability of many chief fire officers to provide the quality of service they regarded as essential. Even after the more prosperous 1960s and 1970s serious disagreements stemming from the poor pay levels and working conditions continued to arise. These came to a head in the national strike of firefighters, 1977-78.

The continuous pattern of excessive hours worked by operational members stemmed mainly from the shortage of recruits and the plethora of new duties being added to their traditional role of fighting fire. With the dramatic expansion of urban communities into former rural districts came a further increase in the number of contemporary hazards, as will be shown below. Those associated with both road traffic and industrial growth were particularly onerous.

Nevertheless, by the 1980s the new regional fire brigade in its resources, organisation and standards of training was firmly founded upon the finest traditions of the former local brigades. When Merseyside County Council was eventually dissolved, 1st April 1986, the Merseyside Civil Defence and Fire Authority took over the responsibility for the management of the brigade. Members of the Authority were elected from the regions' local government bodies and today they oversee its administration from the brigade's headquarters at Hatton Garden, Liverpool.

Within this building maintaining the historic connection with the remarkable achievements of the past are the offices of CFO Andrew E. Best, QFSM, M.I. Fire E. and his deputy, Michael Sullivan. The assistant chief officers for Fire Safety, Operations and Technical Services also operate from this base.

These are assisted by a Senior Staff Officer, a training commandant and a principal fire control officer. The admirable degree of efficiency is reinforced by the well-organised central control room, the staff of which include a communications engineer and special equipment, stores and repairs experts.

Several other highly specialised departments are still housed in Liverpool and add vital support to the everyday smooth running of the Brigade. The former includes the Fire Safety Department, and the Training School, at Storrington Avenue. The latter continues through the commandant to organise many types of training. The special integral features of the building include various styles of roof, window and doors which permit fire simulation exercises to be undertaken. Housing its own appliances, including two fire engines, these can be augmented by other specialist equipment – including emergency tenders and turn-table ladders – as the need arises. Brigade automobile drivers are also offered training there.

Recruits are drawn from across Merseyside. As shown on the Brigade map there were initially five divisions, namely Central, Northern, Southern, Eastern and Western. Their headquarters respectively, were the stations at Bankhall, Buckley Hill, Belle Vale, Parr Stocks Road and Exmouth Street. In September 1992, however, the Merseyside Brigade was re-organised into a Functional Command System. The above divisions were superseded by Operations Command, Technical Command, Fire Safety Command, Personnel and Training Command and finally, Administration Command. Two further units, the Industrial Training Unit, at Banks Road and the Brigade central workshops at Speke Hall Road, are worthy of note. The former opened in 1954, is equipped with a full-sized section of a ship donated by Liverpool ship owners and offers instruction in industrial firefighting. Students from overseas, trainees from foreign brigades and officers and ratings from the merchant navy are among those who have benefitted from its courses.

The Brigade is at the forefront of maintaining an array of

sophisticated technological resources far superior to any at the disposal of its remarkable forerunners. These aids include emergency tender control units, hydraulic platforms, tanker foam tenders, hose-layer units and a radiation decontamination unit.

The demands for assistance by members of the public continues to grow. Throughout the 1970s and 1980s members of the brigade were called upon to help at an annual average in excess of 10,000 small fires. More serious fires in comparison often resulted in annual turnouts in excess of 7,000 in total.

Demands for help other than responding simply to firefighting problems also continued to increase remarkably. Members of the Brigade were generally expected to help at road traffic accidents, when members of the public were trapped in lifts and to examine suspected explosives. Each of these forms of assistance annually involved several hundred turnouts for the brigade. Other equally demanding turnouts included those for removing jewellery, the turning off of water supplies, clearing away flood water and assisting the police in their investigation of crimes. Nor was such assistance restricted to Merseyside for the Brigade, again, on several hundred occasions each year, sent help to adjoining brigades when requested to do so under the mutual assistance agreements. Merseyside, too, also received help in a similar fashion when required.

What of the future? One hundred and fifty years ago the firefighters of Merseyside operated as a mixed collection of private, professional, insurance, retained and volunteer groups. Many brave deeds were undertaken by them – often as they faced overwhelming odds with the most primitive of equipment.

After a long journey in which they and their successors have confronted many 'domes of fire' they have also performed countless courageous acts of selfless sacrifice and outstanding bravery. Those succeeding them have built on their traditions so that a Brigade more professional than ever has emerged. Rigorously trained and using the most advanced of technological aids they now make an inestimable contribution to our local community's well-being.

Ever striving to maintain their high standards of achievement and operational efficiency they are indeed worthy of the finest resources that our local community can provide for them. Not all their endeavours, unfortunately, have been recorded above but hopefully at some future time it may be possible to do so in more detail. What remains without question is that their dedication, expertise and courageous acts of heroism continue to be invaluable to the well-being of the people of Merseyside.

Part Two

The Illustrated History of the Brigades

* * *

Front cover of book:
A Leyland-Rees pump-escape and its crew is shown in the yard of the Central Fire Station, Hatton Garden, c.1925

Back cover of book:
A fire in London Road, Liverpool, c.1980.

Liverpool Town Hall Ablaze, 1795.
Liverpool's magnificent town hall is seen ablaze in 1795. Groups of gallant firefighters struggle to contain the fierce flames. Those involved were dependent on basic equipment such as hand pumps, leather buckets and horse-drawn watercarts.

Birkdale Fire Brigade, c. 1900

This brigade was originally formed in 1876, by volunteers with equipment paid for by local subscribers. Equipment was stored in a shed in Weld Road. The volunteers were summoned by means of a steam hooter at the Compton Road Sewage works. In 1899 the Urban District Council took over and provided a fire station adjacent to the town hall. Two fire engine crews, above, proudly parade outside the town hall. In the foreground the men stand on board the horse-drawn, steam-powered fire engine 'Clissing'. Behind them are their colleagues on the horse-drawn manual engine built by William Rose and Company of Manchester.

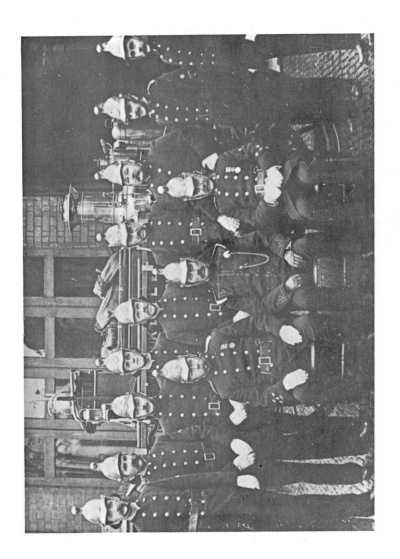

Birkdale UDC Fire Brigade, c. 1900.
The firemen, above, pose in front of their horse-drawn engine, the 'Clissing', built by Shand Mason. Purchased in 1899, it was sold for £90 in 1915 to the Singleton District Council. In 1911 Birkdale District became part of Southport County Borough and five years later the police fire brigade took over Birkdale fire cover. The volunteers were disbanded in 1919 and the Birkdale Fire Station closed.

Birkenhead Fire Brigade, c. 1870

Formed in 1837 as part of the police force, the first Birkenhead firefighters housed their hand-drawn engines in a shed at the Woodside Hotel. In 1843 several insurance companies donated a Merryweather horse- drawn manual which was also stored at the Woodside. The above police firemen with their hand-drawn, hosereel cart were stationed at the main bridewell in Hamilton Street. They were also able to use two horse-drawn manual fire engines and portable ladder escape equipment kept in a large shed at the bridewell.

Birkenhead Horse-drawn Steamer, G. S. Oldham.

By 1889, three fire stations were manned. These were at Hamilton Street, Dale Street and Tranmere and each housed a manual engine, an escape and an ambulance. In 1895 W. J. Monk, from London, was appointed Superintendent and was to lead a fire department outside police control. Above, in 1895, the first horse-drawn steamer, a Merryweather called 'G. S. Oldham', was housed in the Whetstone Lane enginehouse.

Birkenhead Fire Brigade Ambulance, 1900.
Fire escape ladders were stationed at the Central Hospital, in Meadow Lane, at the Workhouse and at the town hall. The Brigade also operated the Ambulance Service in the borough. Number 2 ambulance is seen, above, in the yard at the Whetstone Lane headquarters.

Coronation Celebrations, 1902.
The fire engines decorated for the Coronation of King Edward VII stand at the side of the fire station in Borough Road. The large stables at the centre of the background illustrate the traditional role of horsepower at the time.

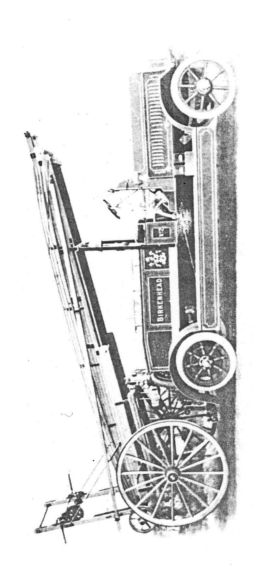

Leyland Fire Engine with Wheeled Escape, c. 1920.
This Leyland-built fire engine was a major new acquisition for the Birkenhead Fire Brigade. Although driver and crew remained exposed in inclement weather they were able to transport the large-wheeled extending ladder escape with them as required.

Fire in Grange Road, Birkenhead, 1920.
Birkenhead's No. 3 motor pump, the 'Laird', is seen at a shop fire in Grange Road, 1920. The pump was a Dennis Tamini, bought in 1915, capable of delivering 500 gallons of water per minute.

Laird Street Fire Station, 1927.
To provide fire cover for the extended borough, which included Bidston, Prenton and Landican, a new district fire station was opened in Laird Street, Birkenhead. The above station was closed when replaced by one at Woodchurch, in 1961. The former station is seen, in 1981, in its new role of youth club centre.

A Leyland Metz Turntable Ladder, 1927.

A Leyland Metz 90-foot Turntable Ladder, 'Halligan', was named in honour of the Fire Brigade Chairman, Councillor Halligan. It was replaced in 1940 by a more modern Leyland Merryweather, also named 'Halligan'.

Annual Inspection, Laird Street, 1937.

The Mayor, Councillor Halligan, and Chief Fire Officer Ball are seen at the annual inspection at Laird Street District Fire Station. The Leyland Pump with registration BG 1404, named the 'James Merrit', and shown above was destroyed by enemy action during an air raid at Prenton, in 1940.

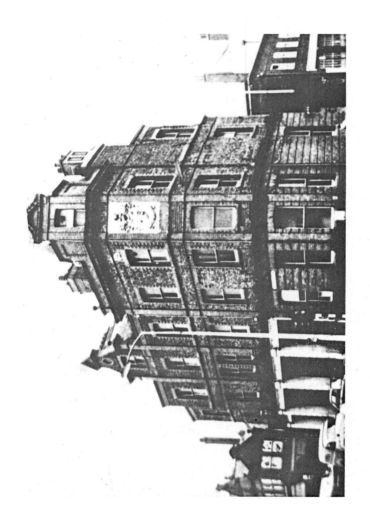

Birkenhead Headquarters, Borough Road, 1938.
Shown above is the extended Borough Road Headquarters. Two bays were added to the frontage together with flats for brigade personnel. Built on the site of a former stables block, there was also a workshop and an ambulance garage at the rear.

Birkenhead Auxiliary Fire Service, 1939.
Members of the Birkenhead Auxiliary Fire Service, formed in 1937, pose in the yard at Whetstone Lane with the 'Laird' and 'Halligan'.

The Birkenhead Appliance Fleet, Borough Road, 1960.
On a quiet Sunday morning the entire Birkenhead appliance fleet is seen outside the Borough Road Technical College.

Woodchurch District Fire Station, 1981.
Above, the Woodchurch District Fire Station, which replaced that in Laird Street, is shown.

Bootle Fire Station, Lower Strand Road, 1898.

In 1870 the Bootle-cum-Linacre town council purchased a hand-drawn hose reel cart to be kept at the Stanley Road Lancashire County Police Station. Four years later a Hall manual engine, the 'Pioneer', was acquired. In 1883 a Merryweather horse-drawn steamer, the 'Bootle', was added. With a full-time engineer to oversee them all three appliances were housed in a large shed in Lower Strand Road. In 1885 a professional fireman, George Parker, was appointed to take charge of a retained brigade at the new Lower Strand Road Station. Above, Superintendent Roberts and his men stand with crews for the Merryweather horse-drawn steamers 'Ibbs', 'Clemmey' and 'Platts' and two hand-drawn escapes.

Fire Appliances, Bootle May Day Parade, 1911.
In 1902 a larger fire station was opened at the corner of Strand Road and Irlam Road. The town's principal appliances are seen, above, decorated for the annual May Day Parade, 1911. Their first motor engine, the 'Ashcroft', was a Merryweather Hatfield with a 50-foot escape and was bought in 1915.

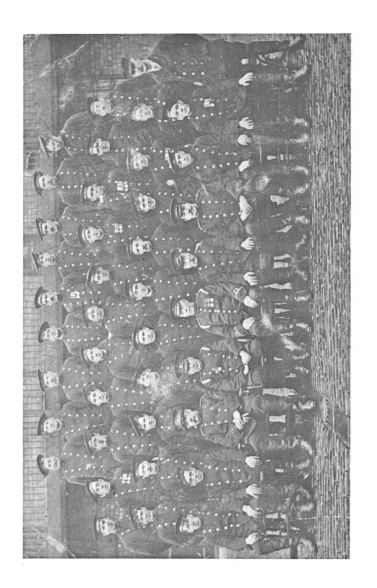

Bootle Fire Brigade Staff, 1924.
Superintendent John Cole, several officers and men from the lower ranks of the fire brigade are seen in the yard of their Strand Road headquarters, 1924. His staff included a second officer, three engineers, twenty eight full-time firemen and a turncock. Although the latter was an employee of the Liverpool Water Department he resided at the fire station.

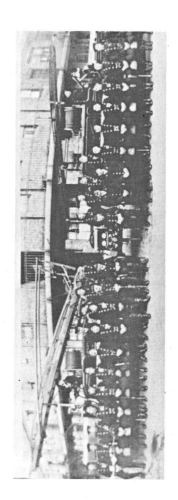

Bootle Brigade Staff and Appliances, c. 1925.
Bootle brigade personnel appear with a variety of appliances, 1925. From left to right these are the Merryweather Aster pump escape, the 'Ashcroft': the Dennis Tamini trailer pump, 'Bellamy', and the Leyland pump, 'Eachus'.

Bootle Leyland Pump, 'Eachus', May Day 1925.
The powerful looking Leyland motor fire engine pump is seen in the foreground. This is seen taking part in the May Day Parade, 1925.

Bootle Fire Brigade Cortège, 1927.
The funeral cortège of CFO Monk, killed in a fall from a blazing cotton warehouse in Pacific Road, passes the Headquarters. Engines and crews from seven fire brigades and Liverpool Salvage Corps attended. In view, right to left, are engines of Wallasey, Bury, Waterloo and Birkenhead.

Bootle Morris Magirus Turntable Ladder, 1928.
Above is the Dennis Morris Magirus, the 'Wolfenden', with turntable ladder. These appliances were usually named in honour of the Mayor or the Chairman of the fire brigade committee.

Bootle Dennis Tamini Pump, Webster, 1929.
This Dennis Tamini 500 g.p.m. pump, the 'Webster', is seen in the Strand Road station yard, 1929. In the background, above, the firemen's flats can also be seen.

Shop Fire, Marsh Lane, Bootle, 1932.
Men of the Brigade attend a fire and explosion at a shop in Marsh Lane, Bootle. Station Officer Mark Edey received fatal injuries as he approached the shop on alighting from the Dennis Pump 'Webster', in foreground. Behind can be seen a Dennis tender of the Liverpool Salvage Corps.

Litherland Rubber Company Fire, 1934.
Fire at the North Western Rubber Company, Hawthorne Road, Litherland. Bootle Fire Brigade had an agreement to attend all fires in Litherland Urban District, from 8th July 1911.

Bootle Fire Brigade, 1949.
The great rubber fire at Gladstone Dock, the view from Rimrose Road.

Bootle's Strand Road Fire Station, 1951.
The east end of Strand Road H.Q., damaged in air raids of 1941 seen when restored with two additional appliance bays. These replaced what was the Chief Officer's living quarters. The large fluorescent light over the bays was automatically illuminated when the bells went down.

RMS Empress of Canada Fire, Gladstone Dock, 1953.
The Salvor pours water into the stricken vessel, the Empress of Canada, after she had turned over onto her side. Written off as a complete loss, she was sold as scrap.

Bootle Dennis Orbitor Appliance, 1970.

A modern fire engine, a Dennis Orbitor, complete with 72-foot hydraulic platform, is seen in the livery of the Bootle Brigade. In 1974, the Strand Road Station became Central 5 Strand Road, of the new Merseyside Fire Brigade. The North East station in Park Lane was replaced by North1, a new station at Buckley Hill, in 1978. Strand Road closed in 1979.

Crosby and Blundellsands Volunteer Fire Brigade, 1890.
The Crosby and Blundellsands Volunteer Brigade, above, became known as the Great Crosby Urban District Fire Brigade in 1894. Though a fire station was provided in the council's yard in College Road, the firefighters were handicapped by their limited equipment. In 1898, for example, fire destroyed the Little Crosby lighthouse and the keeper, his wife and a female guest and the family dog perished. Crosby's firefighters, under Superintendent Watkin Hall and Captain Armstrong lacked an adequate water supply and had to use that pumped through a 1½" domestic pipe.

Crosby Urban District Motor Fire Engine, 1920.
The efficiency of the Crosby Brigade markedly improved with the acquisition, in 1920, of the small Merryweather Aster motor engine, the 'Buckley', shown above.

Crosby Leyland Rees Pump, 1926.
In 1926, under Chief Fire Officer Walter Rigby and his deputy, T. Lovelady, the above Leyland Rees motor turbine pump, TD 7991, was purchased. It carried a 25-foot Ajax extending ladder and could pump 600 gallons per minute of water.

Petrol Tanker Fire, Moor Lane, 1934.
This fire involved a petrol tanker in Moor Lane and emphasized the increasing danger of transporting and storing petroleum. In the following year, 1935, the urban districts of both Great Crosby and Waterloo-with- Seaforth were amalgamated to form the new Borough of Crosby.

Crosby Fire Brigade Inspection, 1935.

The Chief Officer of the Liverpool Salvage Corps, Colonel Colin Lyon, is seen inspecting the new Crosby County Borough Fire Brigade at the Crosby Fire Station. H. Lovelady was chief officer of the new brigade which operated from both College Road Crosby and Prince Street, Waterloo. In total, the brigade operated three Leyland motor fire-engines. In 1941, the National Fire Service took over and on return to local control, in 1948, fire cover was provided from both stations by the Lancashire County Brigade. These stations were eventually superseded, in 1960, by the new station at Crosby Road South.

Estates Fire Brigades. Knowsley Hall Manual Engine, 1799.
This small manual engine, supplied by the Merryweather Company, of London, was used by the Knowsley Hall Estate workers. Later, trained by the Liverpool Fire Brigade, the workers manned a purpose-built fire station in the stables yard. From 1898 they operated a horse-drawn Merryweather steam pump.

Knowsley Hall Ford Model T Pump, c. 1920.
The above appliance, with its 120 g.p.m. pump was purchased in 1920. Estate brigades also operated at Croxteth Hall, for the Earls of Sefton and at Speke Hall for the Watts family. Whenever important guests, such as members of the Royal Family came to reside at the great halls, the Liverpool Fire Brigade provided a pump and crew on twenty four hour stand-by during the Royal presence.

See page 170 for an identical Formby appliance, c.1921

(36a) Formby Fire Brigade.

In 1898 a volunteer fire brigade, under Captain Charters, manned a hand- drawn hose cart and was stationed in Cable Street. When Formby UDC was formed the brigade became part voluntary and part retained with the fire station next to the council offices adjacent to Formby Railway Station. In 1921 when Captain Yelland was in command a Morris 250 g.p.m. motor pump was purchased. In 1931 Captain Ernest Meadows directed the Formby Brigade to deal with fires at J. Barton and Sons in Freshfield, and gorse fires in The Wangs. In 1934 complaints were made regarding the loudness of maroons fired to summon the firemen. Five years later a professional firefighter, CO. David Drummond helped with re-organisation and a new Leyland pump was purchased. Lancashire County fire Brigade provided cover after the NFS was disbanded in 1948. They used a temporary wartime station and later one was built in Church Street. After the 1974 Merseyside Amalgamation this became Station North 6 with one appliance manned 24 hours per day.

Hightown Volunteer Fire Brigade.

The Little Crosby Lighthouse, disastrously destroyed by fire in 1898, was situated west of the River Alt, near the village of Hightown.

Access to the lighthouse for Great Crosby's volunteer brigade had been initially hampered by the lack of any road or track to the building beyond the railway level-crossing at Hightown. As described above when they eventually arrived the volunteers could only dampen the charred ruins of the lighthouse with water pumped through a narrow pipe.

A volunteer fire brigade was established in Hightown, c.1904 as residential development began on the shore-side of the settlement. The Liverpool Salvage Association offered its expertise free of charge to drill the volunteers in the use of some basic equipment which had been purchased from the Liverpool Fire Brigade. Hightown's village representatives had to admit, along with their counterparts in the nearby hamlet of Little Crosby, that they could no longer risk those dangers inherent in having to send for Great Crosby's fire fighters. Too much time, they believed, had been frequently lost in acquiring help from the township.

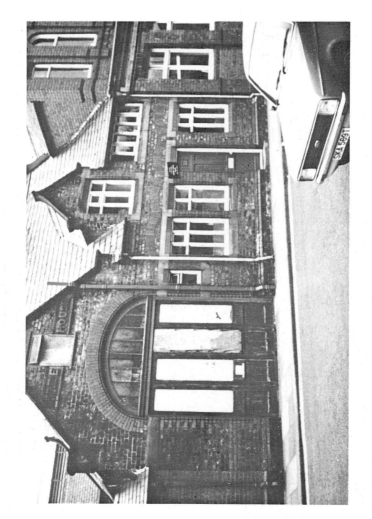

Hoylake's Albert Road Fire Station, 1911-1930.

This photograph, c. 1981, shows the Albert Road Fire Station, Hoylake, operational 1911-30. A volunteer force existed before 1911, for Hoylake and West Kirby, when the Urban District Council formed a retained fire brigade. An honorary superintendent, a captain, sergeant, foreman and twelve firemen became responsible for the UDC horse-drawn Merryweather steam pump housed at the Albert Road base. A smaller station at West Kirby may have supplemented the former station as Brigade rules required that the foreman and four firemen resided in West Kirby.

Hoylake and West Kirby Fire Brigade, c. 1920.

In 1915, Birkenhead Fire Brigade agreed to assist the Urban District Brigade of Hoylake and West Kirby, as the need arose. The latter, pictured above in Stanley Road, Hoylake, proudly stand with their Merryweather Aster Hatfield Motor Pump. This replaced their horse-drawn steamer.

In 1930 the smaller brigade was enlarged under CFO Laird who was aided by the acquisition of a Leyland Cub Pump, a motor ambulance and the new four-bay station built in Station Road.

On the opening day the CFO broke his arm in attempting to start the Merryweather pump and he was unable to take part in the celebrations. When fire broke out, in 1934, at the Queen's Cinema, the combined efforts of the UDC brigade and that of Birkenhead were hampered by strong winds and the cinema was destroyed.

In 1945 when the service was returned by the National Fire Service to local control, the Cheshire County Fire Brigade – operating from Station Road, Hoylake – became responsible for fire cover. From 1974-79 the Merseyside Fire Brigade operated from Hoylake, but the station was closed when a new station at the Concourse, West Kirby was opened.

Huyton-cum-Roby Fire Brigade Station.

The above photograph shows the 'temporary' fire station, beside the church, in Huyton Lane. From 1875 to 1895 the Local Board subscribed £25.00 per annum to the West Derby Volunteer Fire Brigade. Stationed at Derby Lane, Old Swan, the volunteers agreed to attend all the fires in the Board's district. After 1890 they operated with a horse-drawn manual engine from a sub-station in Derby Road, Huyton. Five years later, when the Liverpool City boundary was extended and Liverpool Fire Brigade took over the fire cover, the volunteer brigade was disbanded. The Liverpool firemen took over the Derby Lane Station. Huyton Urban District Council used the Derby Road Station with a volunteer fire brigade, led by a police sergeant to man it.

In 1915 regular assistance from the Liverpool Fire Brigade was agreed to whenever requested by the police sergeant. In 1939 a retained brigade was formed with advice from Whiston's Superintendent Begg. An AFS station was opened in Woolfall Hall, Altmoor Road. Lancashire Fire Brigade, after 1948, took over and operated in the above building until a new one was built opposite it, in 1961.

Litherland Volunteer Fire Brigade, 1914.

The Bootle Fire Brigade attended fires in Litherland until 1891 when the Litherland Board decided to form a volunteer brigade. The new brigade, with equipment supplied by the Board, commenced in 1904. A superintendent and ten firemen operated a hand-drawn, hose cart and escape as shown above. Here personnel and their appliances are seen outside the council offices. Both Litherland's Diamond Match Company and its Liverpool Tanning Company signed cover agreements with the Bootle Brigade, in 1905. Four years later the UDC also approached Bootle to reach an agreement to assist those firemen retained by Litherland. Bootle installed street fire alarms at Bridge Road, Field Lane, Linacre Lane, the Red Lion canal bridge, the Litherland Hotel and at a watchman's hut on the canal. Escape ladders were also positioned in Field Lane, the Litherland Hotel and outside the urinal near the canal bridge.

Liverpool's Superintendent Hewitt and Crew, c. 1865.
Superintendent John Hewitt, centre, and fire crew with the first Merryweather horse-drawn steamer 'Clint' in the yard of the Central Fire Station, Hatton Garden.

Liverpool's Chemical Engine, c. 1896.
A horse-drawn Chemical engine imported from Chicago, U.S.A. It proved an ideal first attendance appliance. Five more were built locally and other fire brigades in the U.K. also took up the idea.

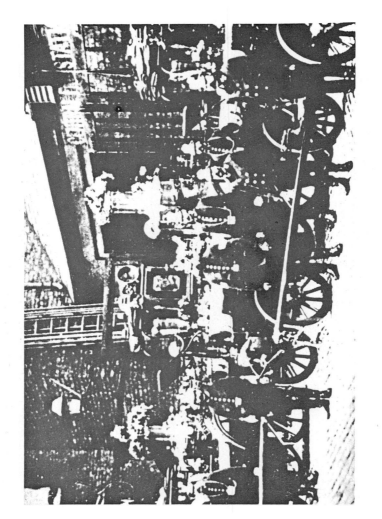

Display of Liverpool Steam Fire Engines, c. 1900.
The florally decorated steamers, Livingston, Holt and Hornby are seen outside the original Liverpool Hatton Garden Fire Station. The acquisition of such steamers was usually marked with a traditional christening ceremony. An integral feature of the event was the naming of such machines, as was the case above, after chairmen of the watch committee.

Liverpool Street Fire Escape, c. 1900.

The set of 'telescopic ladders' comprising this fire escape was mounted on a large wheeled carriage and stationed in George's Crescent. Three men were usually required to move the appliance. Its sliding sections were essential to provide a means of escape from the three-storey buildings in the background and to avoid entanglement with the overhead tram wires shown. When 50-foot horse-drawn escapes were introduced the above type of cumbersome escape was phased out.

Liverpool Merryweather Steamer, Holt, 1899.
The Merryweather steamer Holt capable of 1800 g.p.m. and claimed by makers to be the most powerful land steam fire engine in the world, is shown above.

Daimler Motor Chemical Engine, 1901.
A Daimler motor chemical engine with bodywork by Royal Coachworks, Hope Street, Liverpool. Chief Superintendent J. J. Thomas at the wheel, it was the first petrol engine fire appliance in the United Kingdom.

Mill Street Fire Station, 1904.
Uniformed members of the Fire Brigade stand proudly beside one of Liverpool's six 'Fire King' self-propelled steamers. The Mill Street Station was centred in the heavily populated and industrialised district near the south docks of the seaport. The above sergeant, Henry Anderson, rose to the rank of Chief Inspector. His son Ronald born, in the flat above this station, also served in the Liverpool Brigade as an Inspector. His son is today with the Lancashire County Fire Brigade.

A Liverpool Fire Brigade 'Fire King', 1906.
London's famous Merryweather Company manufactured the self-propelled steamer – shown in mint condition outside Liverpool's Garston Station. Between 1903 and 1906 a total of six were purchased for the Liverpool Fire Brigade. Each, with a steam-powered water pump, was capable of raising 500 gallons per minute. The homes of the firemen are clearly shown to the right of the machine driven by a proud sergeant with distinctive Liver Bird insignia on his uniform.

Magirus Braun Electric Turntable Ladder, 1907.
Magirus Braun battery electric 85-foot turntable ladder. The first mechanically propelled and operated turntable in the United Kingdom seen in Hatton Garden outside the Central Fire Station.

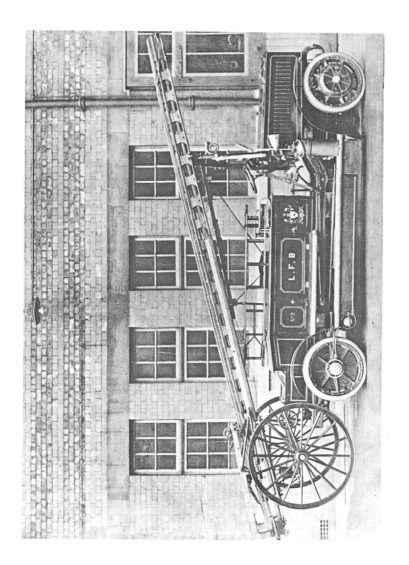

Lohner Porsch Electric Appliance, 1908.
Lohner Porsch, battery electric, 'first turn' appliance with an electric hosereel pump and carrying a Simonis 50-foot lightweight escape. Liverpool had four electric appliances.

Liverpool Fire Brigade Staff Annual Outing, c. 1920.
These firemen await the omnibus stage of their journey – possibly to the Birkenhead water supply source at Lyn Alwen, near Cerrig-y-druidion, North Wales. Their bus, in the Crown Hotel yard, faces the town railway centre, Corwen.

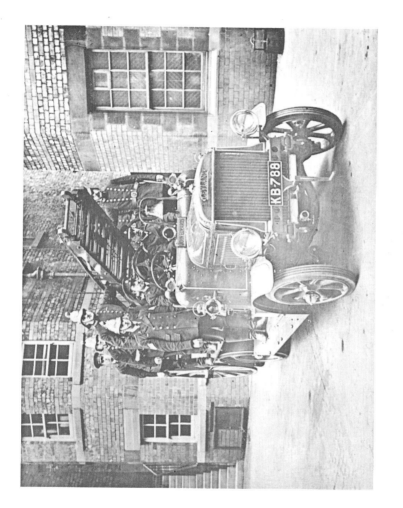

Liverpool Leyland Rees Pump, 1925.
Leyland Rees Pump, with brigade built 50-foot escape, No 11 'John Edwards'. Six of this marque were bought between 1920 and 1929. The nickel-plated helmets shown were replaced by leather pattern in 1926. Seen in the yard at The Central Fire Station, Hatton Garden. The driver, Bob Roberts, was killed on duty at the Mill Road Hospital air raid, 1941.

Liverpool Gamewell Fire Alarm, 1929.
Miss Freda Oakes, daughter of the Chief Officer, demonstrates the use of the newly installed Gamewell Street Fire Alarm System. Unfortunately some post war juveniles needed no such instruction and malicious false alarms rose to such an extent, that the system was removed from 1968 to 69.

Leyland Pyrene Aircrash Tender, 1938.
This Leyland Pyrene Aircrash Tender, designed by CFO, George Oakes, was for service at Banks Road Fire Station, at the edge of the Liverpool Airport.

SS Silver Sandal Fire, 1941.
This is a detailed view of the fire, due to enemy action, aboard the SS Silver Sandal. In the middle of the River Mersey, the ship shows some of its cargo of U.S.A. lease-lend aircraft.

Aircraft in the Mersey Tunnel, 1941.
One of the lease-lend aircraft recovered from the SS Silver Sandal is seen passing through the Queensway Mersey Tunnel, in 1941, en route to Speke.

Liverpool Bomb Crater, Roe Street, 1941.
This dramatic photograph gives an indication of the havoc caused by the enemy bombing of Merseyside during the Second World War, 1939-45. Sergeant John Riley supervises the recovery of the Leyland fire engine from the crater.

Wartime Damage at Liverpool's Centre, 1941.
Some of the war damage after the May Blitz is shown. This was the scene from above the Queen Victoria Monument in Derby Square.

Croxteth Hall Fire, 1949.
Fire at Croxteth Hall, which started in the roof and spread to bedrooms and other rooms on the upper floors before being stopped.

Hendersons' Store Fire, Liverpool, 1960.
Fire, Hendersons' Store, Church Street, Liverpool. Rescue of 11 persons by turntable ladder from the top floor is in progress. 11 others died in the blaze.

Fire at St. Margaret's, Anfield, 1962.
Fire at St. Margaret's, Anfield at the Rocky Lane, Belmont Road corner. Three turntable ladders were used. Unfortunately, the fire had too great a hold and the Church was gutted and demolished and then replaced with a modern style building.

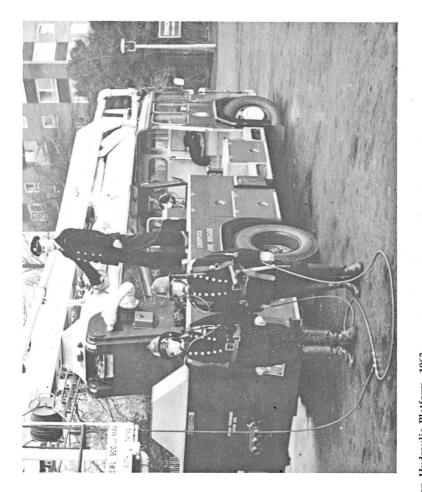

Dennis Simon Hydraulic Platform, 1963. The Brigade pioneered the use of this new type of appliance and fitted compressed air breathing apparatus to the platform, allowing wearers to work at some distance inside a building.

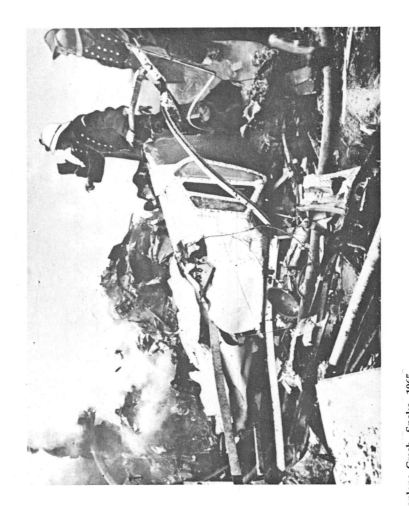

Freight Aeroplane Crash, Speke, 1965.
A freight plane of Cambrian Airways on approach to Liverpool Airport, crashed through the roof of the Mothaks factory on Speke Hall Road. The crew of two and two female factory workers were killed.

River Mersey Tactical Exercise, 1966.
A tactical exercise on the River Mersey. A fireman is lifted by helicopter from a fire-fighting tug for transfer to a vessel on fire. The Liverpool Brigade was equipped to contact ships and RAF aircraft by special radio sets.

Liverpool Salvage Corps, November 1967.
Above, members of the Liverpool Salvage Corps are seen at their Derby Road H.Q. during their annual inspection. The Corps was established after the disastrous Liverpool warehouse fires in 1842. In 1986 the Corps was finally disbanded and its duties were transferred to members of the Merseyside Fire Brigade.

Liverpool Women Firefighters, 1967.
A communication team of Liverpool's Auxiliary Fire Service is shown preparing for their exercise, in 1967, at Moreton-in-Marsh, Gloucestershire.

Liverpool Fire Brigade, Albert Dock, 1969.
An exercise for the Home Office inspector was undertaken at the former Albert Dock offices – now Granada TV studios. The Dock, with its fireproof warehouse altered the course of Victorian Liverpool Firefighting.

No photograph available

Maghull Fire Brigade.

Prior to 1930 a volunteer fire brigade stored a hand-drawn hose cart in a builder's yard. At a meeting of the Parish Council in that year the brigade's efficiency was put to the test when a call for assistance was made from the public 'phone box outside. The tenacious GPO operator failed to persuade the Ormskirk or Southport Brigade to attend. Contact with the Liverpool Salvage Corps who had an agreement with the Liverpool Brigade led to three 'modern' appliances attending the call.

Though the councillors were fined for a false alarm an agreement was reached for cover by Liverpool. The Maghull brigade was disbanded despite protests by Captain J. Alex Smith that it would have attended if the correct procedure had been followed.

Newton-le-Willows Fire Station, Borron Road.
The above photograph shows the fire station in Gas Street, later renamed Borron Road, used between 1920 and 1945. From the former date the Urban District Council operated a retained fire brigade. Equipped with a Leyland Rees 600 g.p.m. pump they frequently dealt with coalpit fires. In 1938 they attended a large fire at Harrisons the cinema furnishers. A Leyland Gwynne pump was purchased in 1939 and the station extended.

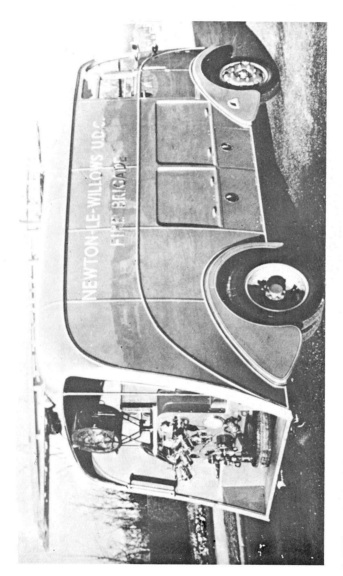

Newton-le-Willows Leyland Gwynne Pump, 1939.
This Leyland Gwynne with Burlington body work and 750 g.p.m. pump, was stationed in the Borron Road extended station. Following the outbreak of war and then the formation of the National Fire Service a four-bay engine house was built in Gas Street. This was later used by the Lancashire County Fire Brigade, until 1962, when a purpose-built building was built opposite the old one. From 1st April 1974 it became Station East 2 of the Merseyside Fire Brigade.

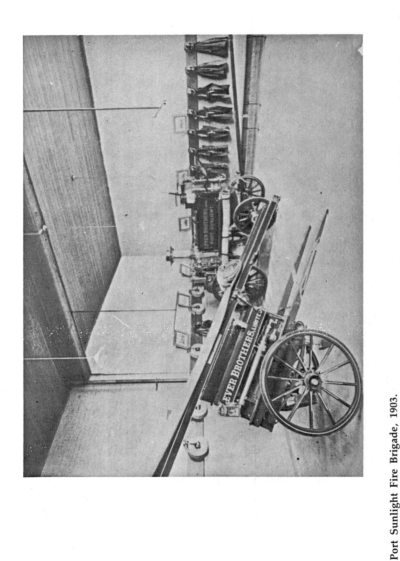

Port Sunlight Fire Brigade, 1903.
In 1888 Lever Brothers built their soap factory which overlooked Bromborough Pool. They organised their own fire brigade under a professional chief officer, H. G. Morrison. With 16 full-time and 12 part-time firemen they had their own single-bay fire station, beside the main entrance to the factory, complete with a horse-drawn steamer. A static pump in the factory boilerhouse used water from the pool to supply fire mains pipes beneath the factory and the adjacent village. The above photograph shows the interior of a second, larger fire station built behind the library and bank.

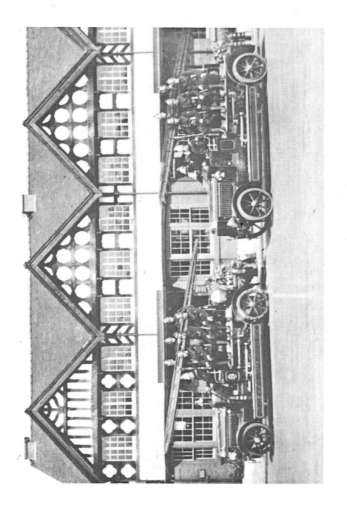

Port Sunlight Fire Brigade Appliances, 1925.
The brigade, from its inception, received calls from residents in the surrounding area. None were refused and after they moved into a new three-bay station, in 1903, extra appliances–including an ambulance–were purchased. The above scene shows Chief Officer E. Stanley, his deputy J. Copeland and third officer, A Bellamy with crews manning their 1915 Leyland pump and the Leyland Rees turbine pump of 1921.

Thatched Cottage Fire, Raby Mere, 1937.
This photograph shows the Port Sunlight fire fighters tackling an incident at a thatched cottage in Raby Mere Village. The brigade's leather tunics were imported from the U.S.A. After 1948, when the NFS was disbanded, there was no fire station, other than Port Sunlight's, nearer than Heswall and Cheshire County Fire Brigade temporarily paid the factory fire fighters to provide cover. In 1959 a new four-bay Cheshire County Fire Station was opened in Dock Road South, Bebington. At the same time, after 71 years of public service, the brigade returned to providing works cover only.

Prescot UDC Fire Brigade, 1899.

The above horse-drawn steamer, supplied by William Rose and Co. of Manchester was named 'Stanley' and is seen in 1899 outside the fire station in Grosvenor Road, Prescot. A reported 16 retained firemen, in 1900, maintained a horse-drawn steamer and a hand-drawn escape which they housed in the two-bay station.

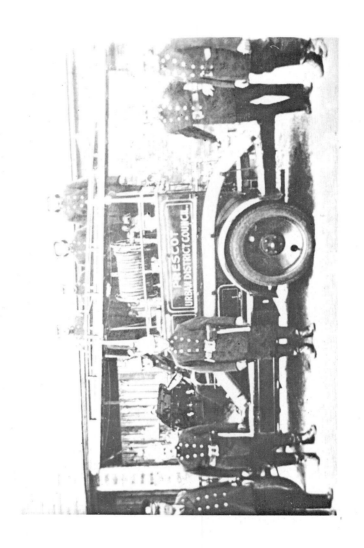

Prescot Morris Gwynne Pump, 1925.
The Morris Gwynne 250 g.p.m. pump, with crew is shown bearing its 25 foot Ajax extension ladder. The vehicle was purchased from John Morris and Son. At this time Superintendent R. Foster and Captain W. Blundell took charge of the brigade.

Shop and Lorry Fire, Eccleston Street, 1938.

In 1936, after complaints of slow responses to fire calls, the directors of BICC Ltd. Prescot asked Whiston Fire Brigade to attend their premises on request-with-payment. Whiston were unable to help so Prescot recruited an extra driver and improved their call out arrangements. The above photograph shows a fire involving a lorry and shop front in Eccleston Street. The Brigade was absorbed, in 1941, by the NFS and not revived after the War. Lancashire Fire Brigade covered Prescot, after 1948, from its Whiston and Huyton stations.

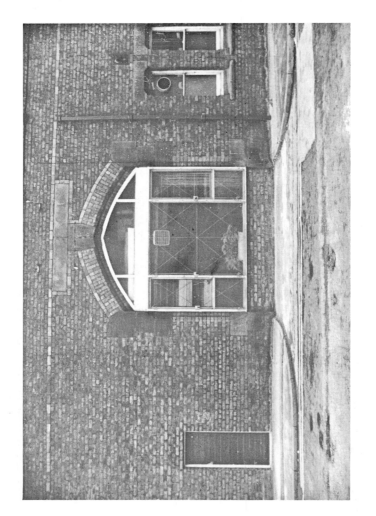

St. Helens Town Hall Fire Station.

By the end of the 1840's a small contingent of the Lancashire Constabulary was based at the St. Helen's Town Hall. In 1858 the Improvement Commissioners set up a fire brigade subcommittee to recruit a body of retained firemen. A fire station was eventually opened in Parade Street with two full-time firemen employed in the stables that also housed a horse-drawn carriage. The above photograph shows the Parade Street headquarters and fire station, with filled-in former entrance to engine house at the rear of the town hall.

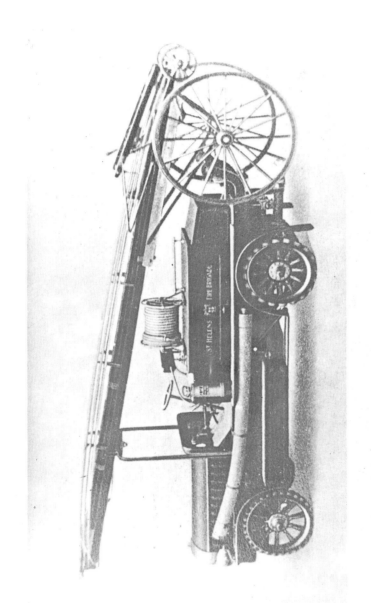

St. Helens Morris Belsize Pump, 1911.

In 1904 Chief Fire Officer Yelland was succeeded by Chief Fire Officer Lyon. Five years later a Shand Mason horse-drawn steamer pump was purchased. The following year a police fire brigade, under Chief Constable Burrows, saw a Sergeant Shaw take charge of fire fighting arrangements. The above photograph shows the Morris Belsize pump escape, 'Dixon-Nuttall', in 1911. This machine was powered by a Forman six-cylinder engine.

St. Helens Town Hall Fire, 1912.
The brigade Shand Mason, steamer is seen in use at the town hall fire, 1912. The newer motor fire engine, the 'Dixon-Nuttall', had failed to start and the steamer 'saved the day'.

St. Helens Gwynne Pump, 1936.

The above Leyland pump escape DJ 7520 was purchased by St. Helens Fire Brigade in 1936. Three years later, at the outbreak of war, J. G. Jessop was Chief Fire Officer. A change from police controlled to independent fire brigade status was then invoked. Three police firemen commenced full-time brigade duties together with civilian recruited firemen. AFS fire stations were located at Wolseley Road, Jackson Street and Highfield Street, Sutton. A reserve control room was set up at Highfield, Scholes Lane.

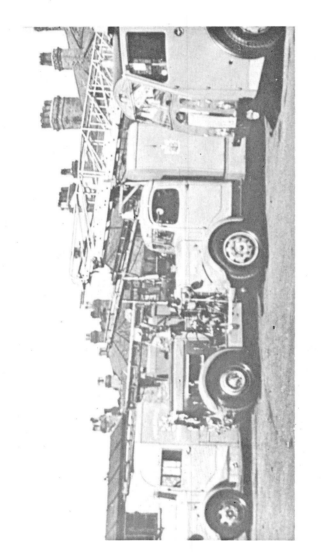

St. Helens Appliance Fleet, 1952.
From 1941-48 the brigade was absorbed into the National Fire Service. It then returned to local control under Chief Fire Officer, J. Chalmers. His full-time staff of 49 had two pumps, a turntable ladder and two trailer pumps. These machines were housed in Parade Street, the police yard and a rented garage in Bickerstaffe Street. The entire appliance fleet is shown, in 1952, in the police yard. Left to right these appliances are an Austin Leyland Tangye Major pump, a Leyland Gwynne pump, an Austin Merryweather pump with 60-foot power operated turntable ladder and a Dennis F12 pump escape.

St. Helens Fire Brigade Appliances, 1959-74.

On 24 August 1959 the Brigade moved into new headquarters at Parr Stocks Road. Parade Street remained as a one pump station until 1972 when it was replaced by a new fire station at Millfields. The above photographs show, to the left, the AEC Merryweather 100 foot turn-table ladder, 1959. To the right is the Albion Carmichael emergency tender, 1974. When Merseyside Fire Brigade commenced in the latter year, the St. Helens headquarters became Station East 1, and Millfields became Station E5.

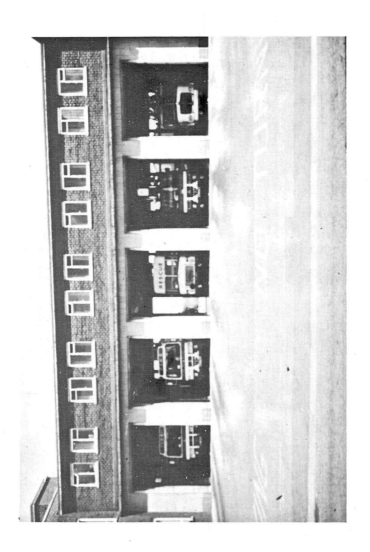

St. Helens Parr Stocks Road Fire Station.
The Parr Stocks Road headquarters opened 24th August 1959 and is shown operational in 1973.

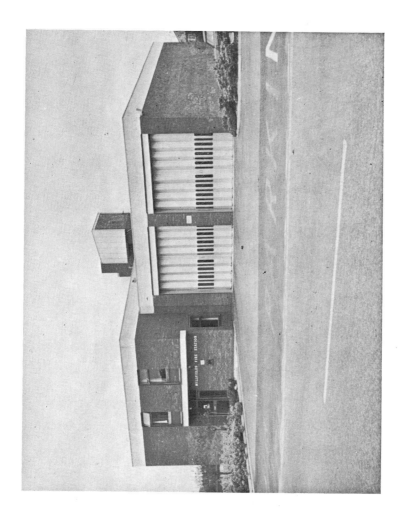

St. Helens Millfields Station 1972.
The new district fire station at Millfields, opened 2nd May 1972.

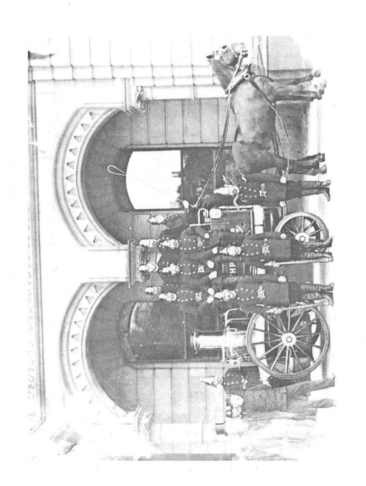

Southport Steam Fire Engine, Lord Street, 1900.
Southport firemen, c. 1900, proudly display their horse-drawn steamer outside the Cambridge Hall, Lord Street. This was a remarkable change from 1845 when a newspaper reported 'on 28th September, fire broke out on the Promenade and as the town has no fire brigade, a horse man was sent to Ormskirk...two engines arrived within one hour and forty minutes'. The house on fire, on a site now occupied by the British Legion's Home, Byng House, was destroyed.

Southport Dennis Pump, 1910.

The first efforts to form a brigade took effect in 1862 when volunteers banded together and a horse-drawn manual engine was bought from Halls of Oldham. Later local police took over the responsibility. Head Constable Kershaw became superintendent of the fire brigade with a police inspector as his deputy. In 1880 their first steamer, a horse-drawn Shand Mason was bought and named 'Nile'. A fire station was erected in the council yard in Tulketh Street.

By 1909 sub fire stations, housing hand-drawn hose and ladder carts were located at Churchtown, Blowick, Crossens, Marshside, Sefton Street and Hart Street. Southport's Dennis Pump with 50-foot wheeled escape – the first of its type on Merseyside – is seen with chemical hose-reel c. 1911.

Fire at the Market Hall, Southport, 1913.
In 1910 in the High Park district, telephones and fire extinguishers were installed in various police houses. These included those of Sergeant Henderson, Norwood Road; P.C. Whitehead in Athol Grove; P.C. Hamer in Sidney Road and P.C. Baldwin in Old Park Lane. When the borough boundary was extended, in 1911, Birkdale was included. The volunteers of the latter brigade – seen above with their Merryweather horse-drawn steamer 'Clissing' at Southport Market Hall fire, 1913 – continued to provide fire brigade and ambulance assistance.

Southport Fire Crew with Dennis Pump, 1924.
With two motorised fire engines in use, by 1919, the Birkdale, Hart Street, Churchtown, Marshside and Sefton Street facilities were closed. Ainsdale too, with its police station, hand-drawn hose cart and ladder was also taken out of service. One of the 'new' Dennis Pumps, with chemical engine and escape ladder are seen above, outside the Southport Visiter newspaper offices.

The Fire Station, Tulketh Street, 1934.
Fire cover was provided from the Tulketh Street Station for the fire at the Opera House, 1929. £37,000 worth of damage was incurred and Police Constable Rigby was seriously injured. In 1932 when there was a large fire at Pleasureland, brigade strength consisted of Deputy Superintendent C. Appleton, five full-time and eight part-time constable firemen and their auxiliaries.

Open Day at Tulketh Street Station, 1934.
Open day at the newly extended Tulketh Street Fire station, with Leyland Rees Pump, in foreground. Displays were given throughout the day.

Leyland Metz Turntable Ladder, 1934.
Leyland Metz 90-foot Turntable Ladder and crew. Superintendent Appleton talks to the Chairman of the Fire Brigade Committee.

Crossens Farm Fire, 1934.
Firemen tackle a farm fire at Crossens.

Southport Auxiliary Fire Service, 1937-45.
In 1940 the Brigade moved into its new Manchester Road headquarters. Inspector C. Appleton, Deputy Sergeant H. Hoyle, 19 full-time fire police constables and 6 part-timers were the complement. Appliances there included two ambulances. The Auxiliary Service – members of which are seen above – formed with the threat of war were housed in some of the former sub-stations.

Chief Fire Officer and Duty Watch, 1948.
Chief Fire Officer Perkins and the duty watch are seen above in front of the Dennis, Big 6 Pump, 'Scott'. In 1948 the reformed Southport County Fire Brigade lost its former police link. When the Brigade merged into the Merseyside Fire Brigade, in 1974 there were 53 full-time and 10 part-time personnel.

The Maurice Evans Pump, 1961.
The family of Fireman Maurice Evans, killed in a fall from a turntable ladder during drill in 1956, pose with the new Dennis Pump named, 'Maurice Evans', in his memory. One Southport pump bears his name to this day.

The Southport Appliance Fleet, 1967.
The entire appliance fleet on the forecourt of Manchester Road headquarters.

Wallasey Firefighters, c. 1891.

In the 1880s a volunteer corps, about seven in number, manned a station in Mill Lane, Liscard. The keys to the station were kept at Smith's Cottage, Dinmore Road. When Wallasey Urban District Council took over the responsibility for fire cover in 1898 a new station was built in Manor Road Liscard, on land donated by a local benefactor. Above, the Home for Aged Mariners, is the setting for personnel with horse-drawn steamer and manual engine and their two hand-drawn escapes.

The Merryweather Steamer, Napier, c. 1891.
All the Wallasey appliances at this time were housed in the Manor Road Station. The 'Napier' – a horse-drawn steamer named after T. W. A. Napier MD., an honorary captain of the brigade – is seen above.

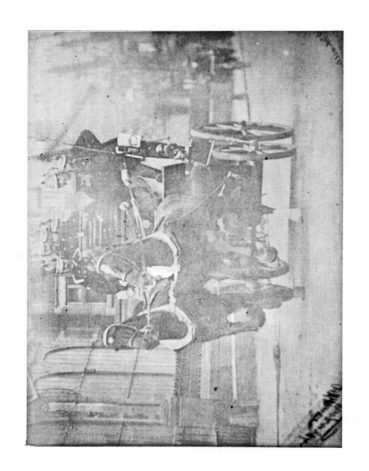

A Wallasey Horse-drawn Escape, 1898.
The above is a rare view of a horse-drawn escape with extending ladder en route to answer a fire call. In 1900, a horse-drawn chemical engine was added. Horses were hired until 1906 when three were bought and kept in stables on the site which later housed the Capital Buildings.

Manor Road Fire Station, 1915.

By 1912 the Wallasey Borough Council had taken responsibility for fire fighting arrangements. A full-time superintendent supervised an engineer, eight firemen, two auxiliary sergeants and their fourteen firemen. They operated from No. 1, the Central Station, No. 2, the sub-station in Brougham Road Seacombe and No. 3, Wallasey Village sub-station. A hand- drawn 50-foot street escape was also positioned in Albion Street. Above, at the Manor Road Station Opening Day a Dennis Pump and Leyland Pump are visible in the engine house.

Manor Road Open Day, 1915.
There were ten town street fire alarms in position by 1912. In that year 46 fire calls were received and 176 ambulance calls. Those in need of aid were variously taken to the Victoria Central Hospital, the Cottage Hospital and Liverpool's Southern Hospital. In 1914 the police took over fire brigade duties and the Manor Road Station was opened a year later. Above, Superintendent Howarth and his staff are seen with their Leyland Pump, No. 2, at the Manor Road Opening Day 1915.

Wallasey Leyland Pump FK4, 1936
In 1941, the Brigade was absorbed into the new National Fire Service and Chief Fire Officer Nicholson became Divisional Officer of the Wirral Area. Above, the Leyland FK4 pump with Ajax extending ladder is seen with Wallasey uniformed personnel under National Fire Service control.

Wallasey Brigade's Dennis Pump, 1970.
Chief Fire Officer Nicholson was succeeded by his deputy Joseph Holt, in 1944. Four years later, Joseph Holt became the new Chief Fire Officer. The Dennis F44 Pump with escape, above is seen in 'Coventry Yellow' livery, 1970.

Fire at New Brighton Tower, 1971.
One of the region's most famous landmarks, New Brighton's Tower Buildings, is shown gutted by fire in 1971. When the Merseyside Fire Brigade was formed, in 1974, Ernest E. Buschenfeld was Chief Fire Officer. His deputy was F. J. Fradley and they supervised more than sixty staff.

Waterloo-with-Seaforth UDC Fire Brigade, 1932.
The Urban District Council, formed in 1894, operated a retained brigade. The latter consisted of council employees under the Urban District Council surveyor. Their station was beside the council offices in Prince Street, Waterloo. In 1913 with the opening of Seaforth's Gladstone Dock, additional equipment including a Leyland Pump was purchased. Above, the 'G. F. Renner', a Leyland Mather and Platt pump registration B 5806, is seen in 1932 after pneumatic tyres had been fitted. Three years later Waterloo was amalgamated with the Great Crosby Urban District Council to form Crosby County Borough.

Old Swan Fire Station, 1898.

A West Derby Volunteer Fire Brigade was formed, in 1865, to serve the townships of West Derby, Wavertree and Toxteth and their rural districts. This brigade was financed by annual subscriptions. The first fire station was in Derby Lane, Old Swan and housed a horse-drawn manual engine. In 1890 a Merryweather horse-drawn steamer was bought and the manual was transferred to a new district fire station at Derby Road, Huyton. After the gutting by fire of Carnatic Hall, Mossley Hill, a third station was opened at Aigburth Vale's, Irwell Street. In 1895 the volunteers were disbanded and Liverpool took over the Derby Lane fire station until 1899 when a larger station – shown above – became operational. Crews with horse-drawn chemical engine, the Merryweather steamer 'Maxwell' and hand-drawn escape are also to be seen above.

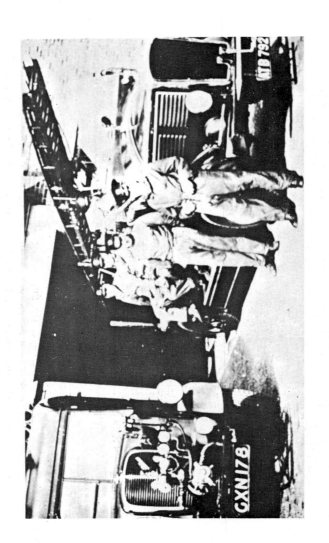

Whiston RDC Fire Brigade, 1935.

Prior to 1915, the Prescot Fire Brigade covered the parish of Whiston. After this year the Rural District Council arranged for the Liverpool Fire Brigade to cover those parishes in the locality, except Whiston. The former included the parishes of Hale, Halewood, Tarbock and Speke. In 1934 the Council resolved to form its own retained brigade to be based at the new Delph Lane fire station. The brigade became operational, with Liverpool Brigade's help when requested, from 20th July 1935. Above we see a Dennis F2 Pump, with Ford Barton Pump with escape, to the right under Lancashire County Fire Brigade control.

Wirral Fire Station, Telegraph Road, Heswall.

Before 1938 there was an agreement with Birkenhead Fire Brigade to attend fires in Heswall. The remainder of the Wirral district relied on the goodwill of Lever Brothers Port Sunlight Brigade. In compliance with The Fire Brigades Act, 1938, the Wirral Urban District Council resolved to form a retained fire brigade. The three-bay fire station in Telegraph Road, Heswall was completed for the brigade in 1939 and is shown above. With the advent of War auxiliary fire stations were opened at Irby Club, Barnston Towers, The Hermitage, School Hill, Pensby Road, Cleaver Sanatorium and Brook Street, Neston. In 1974 The Telegraph Road Station was designated West 3, Heswall.

Merseyside Fire Brigade, Southport, 1977.
Crew members of the Merseyside Fire Brigade fight the fierce blaze at All Saints Church, Park Road, Southport, 1st September 1977.

Factory Fire, Orrell Lane, 1978.
Dense clouds of smoke gather ominously, in 1978, above Reeds Metal Box Company. Many of the dangers of a modern day industrial inferno were encountered in this frightening fire.

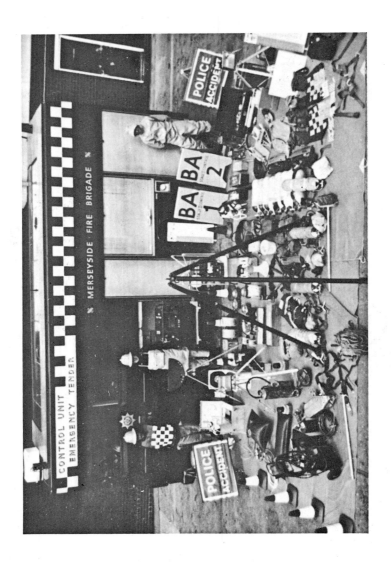

Contents of a Control Unit Emergency Tender, 1980.
A comprehensive array of modern emergency equipment is seen on display outside the Dennis Tender used to transport it.

Area covered by the brigade is 258.9 square miles, of which 2.5 sq.m. are 'HIGH RISK', 5.6 sq.m. 'A' risk, 40.1 sq.m. 'B' risk and 210.7 sq.m. 'C' risk. Equipment includes over 18 miles of hose, 37,000 hydrants, 300 sets of breathing apparatus and 200 ladders.

BRIGADE AREA
Showing Fire Stations
c. 1974

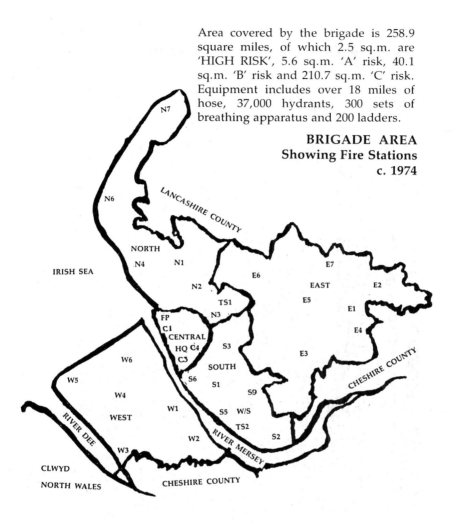

NORTH; 1 Buckley Hill*; 2 Longmoor Lane; 3 Storrington Avenue; 4 Crosby; 6 Formby; 7 Southport

SOUTH; 1 Mather Avenue; 2 Conleach Road; 5 Banks Road; 6 High Park Street; 8 Derby Lane; 9 Belle Vale*

EAST; 1 Parr Stocks Road*; 2 Newton-le-Willows; 3 Huyton; 4 Whiston; 5 Millfields; 6 Kirkby; 7 Rainford

WEST; 1 Exmouth Street*; 2 Bebington; 3 Heswall; 4 Upton; 5 West Kirby; 6 Mill Lane

CENTRAL; 1 Bankhall*; 3 Canning Place; 4 West Derby Road; HQ Headquarters and Control; FP Fire Prevention Department; TS1 Main Training School; TS2 Marine Training Centre; W/S Brigade Central Workshops;

* Denotes Divisional HQ

Glossary of Abbreviations

Personnel

ACFO	Assistant Chief Officer	DO	Divisional Officer
		FCO	Fire Control Officer
ADO	Assistant Divisional Officer	FF	Firefighter
		Fm	Fireman
Aux	Auxiliary	Ins	Inspector (Police)
		LFm	Leading Fireman
Con	Constable	Sgt	Sergeant (Police)
C/Supt	Chief Superintendent	St/O	Station Officer
CFO	Chief Fire Officer	Sub/O	Sub/Officer
DCFO	Deputy Chief Fire Officer	Supt	Superintendent

Appliances

ACT	Air Crash Tender	HWU	Heavy Water Unit
CaV	Canteen Van	LAV	Light and Air Van
ConU	Control Unit	P	Pump
ET	Emergency Tender	PE	Pump-Escape
FoC	Bulk Foam Carrier	PHP	Pump/Hydraulic Platform
FoT	Foam Tender	PP	Portable Pump
GPL	General Purpose Lorry	RRT	River Rescue Unit
HC	Hose Carrier	TrP	Trailer Pump
HL	Hose Layer	TL	Turntable Ladder
HP	Hydraulic Platform	WT	Water Tender

Others

AFS	Auxiliary Fire Service, 1937-1945 and 1953-1968
NFS	National Fire Service, August 1941 – April 1948
CB	County Borough
UDC	Urban District Council

RDC	Rural District Council
GPM	Gallons per Minute
BFB	Birkenhead Fire Brigade
BoFB	Bootle Fire Brigade
Com. Eng.	Communications Engineeer
LAFB	Liverpool Airport Fire Brigade
LFB	Liverpool Fire Brigade
LSC	Liverpool Salvage Corps

Bibliography

I) Manuscript Sources

Much of this material was obtained from two sources:

1) The Liverpool Record Office, William Brown Street, for those of the Commissioners of Watch, Scavengers and Lamps and those of the Watch Committee (1836-1902) relating to Liverpool Fire Police sources.

2) The Merseyside Record Office, Cunard Buildings, Liverpool, for the annual reports of the principal Liverpool fire officers (1926-1973).

II) Parliamentary and Departmental Papers

Royal Commission on Municipal Corporations in England and Wales, First Report, p.p. 1835 xxiii.

Royal Commission on the Health of Towns, First Report, p.p. 1844 xvii.

Select Committee for Protection against Fire in the United Kingdom, 1867.

Select Committee into Metropolitan Fire Brigade, 1876.

Select Committee into Fire Brigades in England and Wales, 1899.

Royal Commission on Fire Brigades and Fire Prevention, 1921.

Departmental Committee on Fire Brigade Services, 1935.

III) Books and Articles

T. C. Barker and J. R. Harris, 'St. Helens, 1750-1900'.

G. V. Blackstone, 'A History of the British Fire Service'.

A. Briggs, 'Victorian Cities'.

W. R. Cockcroft, 'From Cutlasses to Computers; The Police Force in Liverpool 1836-1989'.

W. R. Cockcroft, 'The Albert Dock and Liverpool's Historic Waterfront'.

T. A. Critchely, 'A History of Police in England and Wales, 1900-1966'.

H. Dearden, 'The Fire Raisers'.

'Fire Call' Vols. 1-5.

A. B. Hamilton, 'An Outline of Fire Fighting in England until the Twentieth Century'.

E. W. Hope,   (1) Health at the Gateway.
                (2) Police and Fire Brigade.

Public Health Congress Handbook, (1903).

Q. Hughes, 'Seaport: Architecture and Townscape in Liverpool'.

G. H. Humphrey, 'Liverpool Public Services'.

C. L. Mowat, 'Britain Between the Wars'.

P. Pringle, 'Hue and Cry: The Birth of the British Police'.

J. D. Robertson:

(1) Britain's First Motor Fire Engine in 'Saved', the Magazine of the Fire Services National Museum Trust, Edition 4, Autumn 1989.

(2) Liverpool's Fire Stations: those opened 1866-1973.

(3) Liverpool Salvage Corps, 1842-1984.

(4) The Auxiliary Fire Service on Merseyside, 1937-1941.

B. D. White, 'History of the Corporation of Liverpool, 1835-1914'.

Merseyside's Fire Brigades
Past and Present

Index

Subscribers

A ACFO Brian Airey MFB
    J. W. Austin
    Sub/O R. Arthur MFB

B LFm John Baker MFB
    Mr. Harry Baldam
    Mr. Christopher Baldwin
    Thomas E. Ball MBE
    ADO/Rtd. R. F. Balshaw BFB
    Mr. R. Banyard
    ADO Mike Barton MFB
    Fm. G. F. Bassie MFB
    Janet A. Beesley
    CFO Andrew E. Best Q.F.S.M. M.I.Fire E. MFB
    Bina and P. K. Bhattacharrya
    E. K. Bickley MBE
    Mrs. Alison Blenkinsop
    Sub/O Stephen Blenkinsop MFB
    FCO Stephen Bousfield MFB
    Agnes and Edward Boyle
    DO D. W. Bradbury MFB
    FCOp 8174 Bradshaw MFB
    Mr. Phil Breeze
    Roy Brigden
    Pam and Charles Brundage
    Jim and Margie Byrne

C Vol Fm Charles Carlstrom Canada

FF Christopher Case MFB
Gary Chapman
Mr. Arthur Chidlow
Claughton Fire Protection
Harry Coggins
CFO/Rtd Bobby Collins LAFB
Com. Eng. Edward Connolly MFB
St/O, Rtd. 391 R. Cookson
FF Stanley L. Copeland MFB
SDO M. W. Cotterall Q.F.S.M. MFB
CPS Ltd.
Sub/O 394 Nick Craig MFB
LFm C5C1C4N1 Ron Craig MFB
Mr Ronald G. Croll

D   David Dalzell
Mr G. T. Darby
Sub/O, Rtd Norman J. Davies MFB
M. Dawlings
Keith Day FBSoc.
St/O, Rtd Eric Dickinson MFB

E   Peter Eaton
R. E. Evans

F   Stephen Fagan
Eileen Fenerty
Sub/O D. P. Fenerty MFB
Professor J. Fenerty
C3 1669 John Ferry
Mrs D. Flanagan
Mr. J. Ford
FM 2738 Tony Formela MFB
FF David Foulkes MFB
Mr Raymond Fox
P. H. Fraser
DO G. French MFB

G Mr. Charles D. Garner
   Alan Edward Gartside
   Doris and Trevor Gerrard
   Sub/O, Stephen Gille MFB
   St/O, Rtd Philip Glanister LFB
   St/O Martin Goodwin GI Fire E MFB
   Richard Gordon
   ACFO, Rtd R. Gray Q.F.S.M.
   SDO Tom Green MFB

H Mr P. S. Hardman
   Mr A. Hayward
   Mr D. Healey
   Mr A. Heaps
   St/O Derek Heron MFB
   Mr J. W. Hewett
   Alan Hewitt
   Mr K. Hitchen
   Mr Peter Alan Hobson
   Sub/O John Hodgkiss
   FF 3152 Mark Holland MFB
   Mr S. Hooper
   Dr Louise Horne
   Mrs Lynn Howell
   FF 2067 Hugget MFB
   Michael Thomas Hutton

J Mrs Margaret Jacks
   Sub/O 709 Jamieson MFB
   Mr R. K. Johnson Sec. OCA MFB
   James Johnston
   Joan Jones
   R. C. Jones
   Fm Rtd 741 R. F. Jones
   St/O Paul Joy MFB

K FCO Elizabeth Kermath MFB

L Mr Ivor Lawrence
   Mrs Alice Lawson
   Fm Rtd 792S5 William 'Billy' Lea MFB
   St/O P. N. Lorenzo MFB
   St/O Rtd K. T. R. Lovelady BoFB

M Mr S. A. Mahon
   DO Ian Massie MFB
   FCO Jean McCarthy MFB
   Mr T. K. McClennon
   St/O Rtd Harry McGiveron MFB
   Dr Edward McNamara
   Charles Meighen BoFB MFB Rtd
   Mr J. P. Meighen
   St/O C. T. Melia MFB
   Mr Barry Mellor
   PFCO D. Mitchell MFB
   Michelle Mitchell
   Michael Molloy BA
   Joe Molloy
   John Moncrieff
   Mr A. J. Moore
   Mr Arthur J. Mottram LFB
   Gill Mountfield
   Mr F. A. Mullen
   Sub/O Rtd J. J. Murphy MFB
   John Murray
   Murtec Fire Protection Ltd.
   Alex Myles MFB
   St/O Robert Myron G I Fire E MFB

N Fm Albert Edward Nelson Canada (expatriate)

O LFm Rtd Fred O'Donnell MFB
   St/O Peter O'Donnell MFB
   V. C. O'Donnell
   Helen O'Donovan Admin. MFB

St/O H. O'Neill MFB

P   Mr E. R. Parr
    Fm Rtd 1004 Parr MFB
    LFm 1017 Richard Pendleton MFB
    Phillips Electrical Elec. Contr.
    Sen. DO R. J. Povall MFB
    Sub/O Rtd Walter Powell MFB
    Ken Titherington: Premier Fire (NW) Ltd.
    G. W. Pritchard

R   LSC Rtd Ronald E. Reynolds
    Tony Rice
    Graham Rigby
    Mrs Maxine Roberts
    H. Roberts and Son, Fire Protection
    Mr Gordon Rothwell
    Christopher Thomas Ruane
    LFCOp 8104 Ryland MFB

S   St/O Rtd 1127 J. Saunders
    FF T. Sefton
    Sir John Sergison BA
    John Shallcross
    Mrs E. J. Shannon
    J. P. Shavaksha & Co. Accountants
    Mr and Mrs R. & F. Shepherd MFB
    G. Silcock
    Alan Simmons
    Beryl Smith nee Cottier
    Michael Smith
    M. R. Smith
    Mr Robert Smith
    St/O M. G. Snelham MFB
    David Spicer
    Mr Neil D. Steele
    Mr L. Storey

T   Fm 2030 Alan W. Tagg MFB
    SFCOp 8034 Sue Tate MFB
    Brian John Taylor
    Mr and Mrs G. W. Thompson
    Mr Kenneth Thompson
    W. Tibke LGI Fire E. HMI MFB
    FF 3028 John A. Tierney MFB
    Alan Townley LFB MFB Rtd
    Ken Townley
    Dorothy Turner

U   DO Peter Uttley MFB

W   Sub/O William Walsh MFB
    Sub/O Rtd John Warnock MFB
    Jeffrey B. Watkins
    Mrs Doreen Watts
    Ray Whalley FBS
    DO B. Whittlestone MFB
    Brenda Williams
    Mr Charles Williams
    Douglas Richard Williams
    LFF 1306 Williams MFB
    M. T. Williams
    Fm R. G. Williams MFB
    Robert Gordon Wilson
    Robert Stephen Wilson
    Fm 2932 Mark Winstanley
    Fm 7 Woods St. Helens CBFS
    DO John A. Woosey MFB